The Journey Home

Charles J. Shovlin

TRAFFORD

A Castle Production

Neither the author nor the publisher assumes any responsibility for use or misuse of information contained in this book.

Note for Librarians: A cataloguing record for this book is available from Library and Archives Canada at www.collectionscanada.ca/amicus/index-e.html
ISBN 1-4120-6602-6

Printed in Victoria, BC, Canada. Printed on paper with minimum 30% recycled fibre. Trafford's print shop runs on "green energy" from solar, wind and other environmentally-friendly power sources.

Offices in Canada, USA, Ireland and UK
This book was published *on-demand* in cooperation with Trafford Publishing. On-demand publishing is a unique process and service of making a book available for retail sale to the public taking advantage of on-demand manufacturing and Internet marketing. On-demand publishing includes promotions, retail sales, manufacturing, order fulfilment, accounting and collecting royalties on behalf of the author.

Book sales for North America and international:
Trafford Publishing, 6E–2333 Government St.,
Victoria, BC v8t 4p4 CANADA
phone 250 383 6864 (toll-free 1 888 232 4444)
fax 250 383 6804; email to orders@trafford.com
Book sales in Europe:
Trafford Publishing (uk) Ltd., Enterprise House, Wistaston Road Business Centre,
Wistaston Road, Crewe, Cheshire cw2 7rp UNITED KINGDOM
phone 01270 251 396 (local rate 0845 230 9601)
facsimile 01270 254 983; orders.uk@trafford.com
Order online at:
trafford.com/05-1513

10 9 8 7 6

Dedication

I dedicate this book to all those seen, and unseen, forces that have crossed my path and guided me on this journey.

To Mary

With all the best wishes

of possible Energy

Be safe and be happy

Charles

Contents

Part Two–Strange Happenings

Foreword

Why feel old, just because time passes?

I remember saying to a good friend and student of mine in Wales on a Taiji seminar, that I would use these words of inspiration in my third and final book, The Journey Home.

Here is my story: and the story of the Castle that changed

my life and the lives of others who were fortunate enough to share the experience with me, both in the Castle and as regards the new-found talents it brought me. I suppose I've always been a deep thinker, someone with an inquisitive mind – well perhaps a little more so than the rest of the family. They say there's a black sheep in every family and I suppose I did come across to the rest of the gang as being somewhat strange. After all I shaved my head when I

Dave Sullivan & myself on holidays in Wales 2000.

was seventeen years of age, during my fourth year in the comprehensive school in Glenties.

I enjoyed every day I spent there and regarded it as my second home. Indeed perhaps it was home, as I was one of the last babies born on those very grounds, on the 24th of June 1958. The comprehensive school now stands on the site of the old Glenties Hospital.

Glenties comprehensive school

The school planted in me the hunger for knowledge and the love of learning that has thankfully stayed with me to this present day.

Old Glenties Hospital

I grew up on a small farm in the townland of Kilraine in southwest Donegal, near the picturesque village of Glenties. Kilraine has roots going back for hundreds of years and is steeped in spiritual history and spiritual values, which would later give me the grounding to develop my hidden potential. Kilraine takes its name from Saint Riadhain, who built a Church there in the late sixth century.

The house where I was reared

Tradition refers to her as one of the three saintly sisters, of whom St Patrick is said to have prophesied would found three churches, 'where the salmon leap and the deer frisk around'. This description would have surely have fitted Kilraine in those days. St Riadhain is said to have blessed a well there, known from then on as St Riadhain's Well.

St. Riadhain's Well

Pilgrims recently restored it and its water is as clear now as it was when it was a popular pilgrimage shrine. The local graveyard marks the precise spot where St Riadhain built her Church and the saint's tradition was carried on by a whole host of spiritual teachers who came after her to continue her work. It goes on to the present day.

I suppose when one comes from a place that has had its share of priests, nuns, nurses, scholars, teachers, a bishop and a cardinal, – not to mention healers, it would be strange if one did not show an interest in it and share in its mystic past. One of the most famous sons of the townland of Kilraine was my late granduncle Dr Michael O' Donnell.

Dr. Micheal O' Donnell
1882 - 1944

He in turn had an even more famous cousin, the late Cardinal Patrick O' Donnell.

Dr Michael, as he was affectionately known, was one of the most brilliant men born in this country, a professor of Moral Theology in Maynooth – a man with an astounding mind and prodigious memory. It was said that if the code of Canon Law was destroyed he could rewrite it from memory. I

Cardinal Patrick O' Donnell
d. 1927

would not have known anything about Dr Michael were it not for my late mother.

She told me everything about him and the Castle, the house he built for his parents. She told me everything she could about his healing work and lots of interesting stories about the gift of healing in general, although none of this made sense to me until later years. She did not tell me how to develop the gift or indeed if I was the one in the family who would have it. All of this came later. But I think my mother may have had a fair idea because to me she appeared somewhat psychic.

My mother Annie Kennedy Shovlin

I was the one out of the seven of us – two girls and five boys, one of whom died before I was born – whom my mother told about other worlds or places that she could visit in her mind. Sadly she could not develop her own healing gift, or perhaps even completely understand it, partly because of her religious background. She was torn between religion and what she perceived to be superstition, as so many were at that time, because of the church's domineering role. She suffered from multiple sclerosis (M.S.), which is a blockage of the body's energy system. I found this out some years later when I began working as a healer myself. Although I looked after her as well as I could, she passed on early in life, perhaps to leave room for my gift to blossom. This took on a somewhat different slant to that of my late granduncle, to suit the times in which we now live.

My great grandparents James & Catherine O' Donnell Kilraine

Although the gift of healing comes from my mother's side of the family,

Back: Eileen & Peter Kennedy
Front: Annie Kennedy Shovlin, Mary Kennedy (nee O' Donnell), Rose Kennedy (Sr Aquinas) and Kathleen Kennedy Kirk

I also owe a lot to my father's side, from which I get the strength to carry the gift.

My great grandparents on my father's side of the family, Mr. & Mrs George Byrne

This helps me to keep both feet firmly on the ground. If it were not for my father I would not have started searching in the first place. He was also the one who started me exercising.

My grandparents on my father's side of the family, Frank Shovlin and Mary Ann Shovlin

My father was a tradesman, and a good one; I later discovered this for myself, when he built my present family home in his early seventies. He was a very fit man and blessed with good health all his life. When he came in from a day's work sometimes he would teach us some exercises, or what he called tricks. I seemed to be the one who caught on quickly. I had no problem

My Father Peter Shovlin

learning these exercises because I was naturally fit myself and had the interest. Later they would play an important part in my martial arts journey. Looking back now, some thirty years on, I see my life as a journey of self-discovery.

I have a lot to be grateful for to both my parents. After all they reared six of us on a small farm with little or no money coming into the house. It was hard work making a living back in the sixties.

What with helping to save the turf and hay in the summer, milking the cows and feeding the outdoor animals in the winter, we all had our part to play in keeping body and soul together. But that was the way it was back then for most families, and looking back now it was not so bad. I recall many memories of my childhood days, some happy, some not so happy. I remember aunts and uncles coming and going bringing us sweets and clothes and nice things and questioning us about schoolwork. I used to dread being asked to spell out words or to make sums up in my head. I hated that and I couldn't wait for them to leave. I have memories too of sitting up with sick cows and waiting for the arrival of a new calf, wondering what name would you call

Mammy, Peter, Frank, Michael, and Daddy at the harvest in the sixties

it, if you could stake your claim on it before the rest of the gang beat you to it.

I hated the harvest, as it put so much pressure on us. All the farm work had to be done by hand back then, not like now. It was very hard work and it took up most of the summer holidays. However, I used to look forward to us all getting a new pair of sandals in the summer and a pair of wellingtons in the winter. We had to walk to school then.

Birthday times too were very special. Well, mine was anyway, because I have the nicest godparents anyone could ask for. Every birthday without fail they remembered me. My mother remarked that I was 'born lucky' but there were loads of sad times to balance things out. The family growing up and moving on brought its sadness – as it does to families. I remember one such instance when my second sister Mary had to go to live with one of our aunts. She had to go to school from my aunt's and it nearly broke my heart. Mary was the one who had taken care of me when my mother fell sick and was diagnosed with multiple sclerosis, (M.S.).

But amidst all this sadness and hard work there were some very funny times as well that kept us going. One such time that sticks in my mind was when my parents would go visiting friends. The rest of us would play tricks on the neighbour who was looking after us. It was usually a man that was left to look after us. I remember well my older brothers Frank and Michael filling this man's pipe with turf mould instead of tobacco. He would go mad. He would always forgive us and return, only to have another trick played on him again the next time round. Looking back now it seems all so innocent and such good fun. I suppose it was all planned for a purpose, as all our lives are;

nothing happens by chance. Sure enough when the time came for me to develop my genetic ability, it was far from by chance that I went into my very first martial arts school in Killybegs under the guidance of Plunket Smith. I did not know then that it would open a doorway for me that would set me on a journey of self-discovery – the journey home – that I will share with you in the pages of this book.

1

Fondest memories

I was the youngest of the family and unable to walk until three years of age. This must have put extra strain not alone on myself but on the rest of the family. I remember my mother telling me that she worried a lot if I was ever going to walk. A neighbour told her not to worry – that I would walk plenty yet. Although I was a late developer, somehow it never held me back. For one thing it probably planted in me the determination to keep on going.

One thing that I've always been blessed with is a good memory. It has always helped me greatly during my life. The fondest memory I have is of that day when I took my first steps. I will never forget the look on my parents' faces, and the excitement it brought to myself and to the whole family. I remember been asked one time in an interview when had I started training, and jokingly I replied, 'I started when I was three.' Another fond memory I have (I suppose like a lot of other people) is of the day I started school. I went to Drumnacrosh local national school at the age of five.

*This is myself with the pupils of St Riadhian's NS. (Doing
Skip-atom week)*

I remember it as if it was yesterday. My sister Mary took me by
the hand up the road, as we lived only a short distance from the
school. I was a little bit frightened at first. The school felt so big to
me then. The teachers were very nice
and kind. For the first few days my
teacher gave me treats of Marietta
biscuits! Sure I thought school was
a great place. School indeed was a
great place, as I learned new games
and developed new interests there.
Speaking of games, I wasn't really
into sports at all, as I used to spend a
lot of time daydreaming, something
that's encouraged in modern-day

My sister Mary

therapy. Once I gave a whole workshop on the subject myself
– on how to expand the mind and release the mind's energies,
which if you like is daydreaming. It's a funny old world, isn't it?

At the age of thirteen I left the national school and went to the comprehensive school in Glenties, The 'Comp', as it was known locally. My father wasn't going to send me to secondary school; he felt that I'd be needed at home to help out with the farm work and to look after my mother, who at this time was in very poor health. But my mother insisted that I should go to the 'Comp', my being the youngest and all that, and because there was only myself and my sister Mary now left to educate. The rest of the gang were all in good jobs. Secondary school proved a little difficult at first, as I was somewhat of a slow learner then. However, thanks to the wonderful teachers and fellow-students I survived, and came out of it much better than I went in. Although I spent five years there, I'm afraid I didn't receive any medals for sporting activities there either. But I was quite popular there and always seemed to have lots of friends supporting me in the other antics I managed to get up to. Looking at it now, I suppose these were for me a way of escaping from all my responsibilities.

One memory that stands out clearly in my mind is of the time long hair was in fashion. All the senior boys were starting to grow their hair long as part of the trend, as we didn't have to wear uniforms back then. So everybody was jumping on the bandwagon and fashion was a free-for-all. But this did not win any favours with the principal of the school. No wonder perhaps, as most of us boys took bad care of our hair and a lot of the time it would look dirty and scruffy. The principal saw this as a poor reflection on the school. He tried to stamp the fashion out immediately, before it took root. As I was no different from the rest of the boys I started to grow my hair long too. One evening as I was going to catch my bus home, the principal saw his opportunity. He tapped me on the shoulder and told me to get my hair cut for Monday. I didn't disobey him and got it cut as he requested, but perhaps a little too short. This was just for a laugh, as I was full of antics. I came in the following Monday morning with my head shaved. You can imagine the commotion I caused. I was suspended for a few days, but you may well believe that I was quite popular in the school after that. The principal never mentioned hair again.

At others times too I would dress up in my own particular fashion – waistcoats and what have you, for a laugh. This was the way I had of expressing myself then, while the rest of the boys and girls would perhaps express themselves through the school games, for instance playing basketball or football. I was never too fond of sport at school. Nor was there much sport going on at home apart from running errands to the local shop and learning my father's tricks like jumping the poker and going through the broom. Sometimes though, I would steal the school boxing gloves and have a friendly punch-up with the lads at break time. At that time I was developing an interest in the martial arts, and always enjoyed a good punch-up. Some of my old schoolmates and I still talk about our schooldays when we get together and even yet it gives us all a good laugh.

The farm work certainly kept me fit and strong. Another thing I have to be grateful for is dancing at the local dances, which really kept me in good physical shape. Indeed later on dancing went hand-and-hand with my martial arts training and made it much easier for me to grasp. Looking at it now I suppose we must have been so easy to rear back then, as luckily there was very little drink or drugs in those days – only the rock music. And once bands like Deep Purple or Status Quo hit you (these were my favourites) sure it was a drug in itself. So it was this combination of three things – dancing, martial arts and working at home which shaped me in so many ways, and which stands to me to this present day.

Although the seventies brought huge responsibilities they were still wonderful years. It was a time of change in my life, with the discovery of newfound interests, challenges, and talents.

2

A Plan for Us All

Although, we did not have a television, as my father had no time for that sort of thing. I used to see David Carradine, in full flight, in our neighbours' house. It wasn't until I saw Enter the Dragon that I got interested in the martial arts, through the films of Bruce Lee. At that time if you weren't involved in football, you were the odd one out. I had two left feet – I did not even own a football – but kick and punch I did, thanks to my hero Bruce Lee. I was learning in any way I could. I must have been buying three to four magazines a month, not to mention Kung Fu Monthly, that came out after the death of Bruce Lee.

By the time I was fifteen, I had a nice wee school going on in the barn, showing off my new physical and martial skills to my friends, or to anyone that showed an interest. My father never encouraged my new-found interest; he thought, it was taking up too much of my time. Many a time he chased me out of the barn for scaring the cows, as I was giving the punch bag everything I had. Later on, after my mother passed away, I fed it with my anger and frustrations. Even a priest who was a close friend of the family noticed that I had a lot of anger in me, because I grew up with a sick mother, and was left to take care of her. The rest of the family were all grown up by now, away, married or at college, so the burden of looking after my mother seemed to be left to me. Indeed we all had our part to play there. I'm sure the rest of the family would have their own story to tell. This is my story, and looking back now, I realise that the task of looking after my mother carved me for the future. It gave me commitment, compassion and understanding in how to deal with the sick.

Before I got involved with the martial arts, this priest advised me to get into sports. He said this would help me to channel my anger. I took his advice and thankfully, I never looked back. Although, my mother was sick, I never looked on her as a burden. Sometimes I felt the pressure of it all, and she would console me in her own quiet way. She told me that, I would be well rewarded for my efforts some day. She had a wonderful mind, and was the only person who encouraged me greatly in my training. She would put hot coals in a bucket for me to heat sand. I was developing the 'iron hand technique", to strengthen my palms, to break tiles. Little did I think what I'd eventually be using my hands for? When I was still very young, my mother told me, that people would come to me for my talents. But it was not until long after her death, that I knew what she meant.

The martial arts came to an end, (or so I thought) and I left school, and headed to London. They say that faraway hills look green; well, I lasted only two weeks in London. I was like a tree that had lost its roots. I am a countryman at heart and I couldn't wait to get back home. However I was not yet ready to settle, so after a short spell at home, I upped sticks again and joined the army. This proved to be another disaster. I did not finish my training and after sixteen weeks got, got an honourable discharge. I went home again. This time I struck it lucky and landed a job in Bord Na Mona. I settled down, and got married to my darling wife Grace. We had four boys: Hugh, Peter, Daniel, and Martin.

Sadly, Martin was not for this world and he died after two days.

Grace Shovlin, Peter Shovlin, Hugh Shovlin and Daniel Shovlin

I loved my job in Bord Na Mona. The work was outdoors with plenty of fresh air and it suited me down to the ground. However, through no fault of my own, the job came to an end within a few months of my marriage, I was made redundant. I've always managed to keep my head above water and things worked out fine.

During the early years of my marriage martial arts were never far from my mind. I was all the time training at one thing or another, like skipping or cross-country running. The punch bag would go up from time to time. As everyone knows, marriage is not a bed of roses. So when things stirred up, I would take my emotions out on the punch bag and things would be grand again. I remember once making the comment at a pre-marriage course, that all newly married couples should have a punch bag. Well whatever about the punch bag, Grace and I are still together. I went back into martial arts again, this time in full swing. This time it would change my life forever.

I started studying and training in earnest, going from one teacher to another. Teachers, like Onie Curran, and Josie Kyles, deserve a lot of credit and thanks for introducing martial arts to Donegal. Today it has taken a strong foothold, in the external and internal styles. I was going from one class to another, learning in any way I could. In the early 1980s, there was very little in the way of organised classes around, until Josie Murray founded the "Rosses Ju-jitsu Club." Josie was then a black belt in ju-jitsu and he started up classes in Dungloe.

Training with Josie Murray

I started training with Josie and we became the best of friends, on and off the mat. We had a great school there and trained every Tuesday night without fail.

Training in Josie club 1983

Josie would often let me take the classes. This I have to thank him for, as it gave me the confidence to teach. After seven years, I left the club and went to train with the big clubs in Belfast, under the World Ju-Jitsu Federation. I trained regularly in Belfast until 1990.

Training with the Masters
Training in Belfast with the World Ju-Jitsu Federation.

Nineteen-ninety was one of those years that everything seemed to happen. It was a terrible year for my family and myself. I had my appendix removed at Easter of that year. This made the cutting of the turf almost impossible; a job I loved doing. To crown it all we lost our fourth son Martin. At that point I was going to give up my martial arts training forever. I suppose God has a way of keeping us going and somehow has a plan for us all. Although my wife Grace had little strength left by now, she insisted on the day of Martin's funeral, that I was not to give up my black belt training. I was due to be graded in early October, the same year. "Do it for me and for Martin," are the only words, I remember of that horrible day. I went to Belfast and finished my training and on the 25th of October I was graded my black belt in Ju-Jitsu by Professor Robert Clark, 9th Dan, of the World Ju-Jitsu Federation, Liverpool.

This was a wonderful experience for myself, one that I will never forget.

I was graded my black belt

3

No Time for Gurus

Often I would stay overnight in Belfast with my good friend Alan and his wife Anna, Anna later wrote a story about the Castle and myself (some four years later). I returned from

My Ju- Jitsu club in Glenties.

Belfast and opened up my own Ju- Jitsu club in Glenties, which lasted four years.

Although I was teaching Ju- Jitsu long before I opened my own club, my health was declining between the late 1980s and the early 1990s. I looked great on the outside, but inside, where it counts, my liver was giving me bother. So I started to look at my own health, and began to study books on the ancient art of Tai-Chi and Qi- Gong, (sometimes spelt Chee Gung) Tai-Chi is a household name in China, and is associated with a broad range of mental and physical exercises generally regarded as beneficial to health maintenance and health improvement. More than ten million people there practise it.

Qi-Gong dates back to the Quing Dynasties of 960–1911 AD. It was used in connection with mysticism, and many people shrugged it off as superstition, but with advances in modern science and physics, over the past century, there was a resurgence of interest in it. Qi-Gong has been researched in the light of modern science and many of the exercises, which did result from superstition, have been tested and discarded but others have been retained. So in China today Qi-Gong clinics have been set up to study and teach Qi-Gong and treat diseases.

Some common results of practising Qi- Gong are: gain in overall health; increase in energy and efficiency; decrease in sleep requirements while sleep quality increases; decrease in hunger and food intake; increased capacity to handle stress and be relaxed; increased ability to enjoy peace of mind and relationships with others; improved self-confidence, self-esteem and overall quality of life. These benefits also apply to Tai-Chi or the old spelling Taiji, which is, if you like, all the Qi-Gong exercises strung together in meditation and therefore known as 'moving meditation'.

I first remember seeing twelve exercises in The Book of Kung –Fu, which I still have. They had something to do with proper breathing and to do with placing your tongue against the roof of your mouth. Later on I learned it was Qi Gong. I dug this book out again from the huge collection of books and videos I had now collected; by people like Earle Montaigue, head of the World's Taiji Boxing Association, Australia, and Danny Connors from Manchester, whose book and video I got on the 24-step Tai-Chi Ch, aun. I started learning it myself with great difficulty, as Tai-Chi is almost impossible to learn from a book. However, I had the good fortune to meet with Danny later at a Tai-Chi seminar in Derry.

Tai-Chi seminar in Derry with the late Danny Connors

He helped to correct me on the 24 steps Tai-Chi Ch, aun. Later I went on to develop my own style and made my own video of it some years later, called Tai-Chi for Everyone.

At this time I began to study in earnest everything I could get my hands on, letting go of the ego. It's funny how easy it is to let go of one's ego when one is in poor health. I somehow knew that my health was failing. I also knew I could do this, as I had already strengthened my lungs and breathing by doing physical exercises when I was thirteen years of age. I had nearly died from pneumonia that year, and because of that illness I knew that I had the willpower, determination and commitment to carry it through.

Long before I went training in Belfast I was well versed not alone on the external arts – karate, judo, and ju-jitsu – but on the internal arts such as Tai-Chi, and Qi-Gong. As I advanced into the 1990s my hunger was still growing in the search for more knowledge on the arts of Tai-Chi and Qi-Gong and their healing properties. I even had books now on two of the world's renowned healers, Harry Edwards and Betty Shine. At the same time my interest in the external arts was slowly declining. To my surprise and to the surprise of my doctors my health was on the up.

I started to notice my body getting much lighter although I was still the same weight. I seemed to be lighter in step. I could do with less food and fewer hours of sleep and my wardrobe was getting lighter and lighter too, as my energy level went up. I could now were the same kind of clothes in winter as in summer, colds and flu's occurred less and less. I could even draw energy into my body from the earth by the practice of Tai-Chi, Qi-Gong and meditation. As one doctor puts it, 'Well, Charlie, whatever you're doing it seems to be working', and he and one of his colleagues got me to demonstrate Tai-Chi for them. It was later discovered that I had a rare disease called ellipticsytosis of the liver. In other words I had hereditary jaundice. Yes, once again my ancestors came to the rescue – this time on my father's side of the family. I realised from looking after my mother how important it is to have good health.

I started to introduce the Qi-Gong internal arts into my Ju-Jitsu class. I started to get more involved with the health side of things. My teaching and training took on a different slant to that of my early days. My students, loyal as they were, were not ready for this guru who was teaching them more about moral issues than about combat issues. Finally we went our separate ways. However, I was still searching for an answer or for something or someone to guide me, someone to show me the path. I knew I had a greater purpose to fulfil as my mother's predictions were starting to make a little sense by now.

4

Another journey

All this time I was teaching lots of people, in and out of clubs, both in small groups and in private classes. I was burning the midnight oil, staying up late at weekends writing to this and that organisation all over the world. As they say God loves a trier. So one day, to my surprise, I got a letter in all the way from

Erle and myself at a workshop in Sligo 2005

Australia from Erle Montaigue head of the World's Taiji Boxing Association, whom at that time I had never met.

The letter stated that Stuart Lee Marseny, also an Australian chief instructor of the WTBA, was at that time in Europe. He would give me a call if I were interested. I immediately wrote back; it's funny how fate had a way of bringing us together when the time was right. The letter went half way around the world, eventually finding Stuart in Waterford in the south of Ireland, where he was on holidays with his wife and family. I met Stuart and his family in July 1993 and immediately struck up a kinship with him.

Stuart, Sheila and myself

Stuart was one of those rare and special individuals one comes across only now and again in one's lifetime. He was a remarkable teacher and philosopher of the internal arts with a huge amount of knowledge and confidence to go with his teachings. I'm grateful he passed on some of those skills to me. As well as teaching me the first third of the Yang Cheng- Fu Taiji long form, he held a workshop locally in Ardara that year. He was quite excited on hearing about the gift of healing, which was in my ancestral past. On his departure he gave me some qualifications to enable me to teach a little Tai-chi and Qi Gong. He also taught me some

Myself doing Tai-Chi 1993

wonderful Qi-Gong postures, which I was to study, and do in the bare feet, until we would meet again.

This I found difficult at first, but it was to help me to develop my healing potential, to further opening up my channels, and help me cope with the extra flow of energy my body was now receiving. I was drawing energy from all quarters. He also offered me a three-months' scholarship in Australia to learn all there was to know about the internal arts – their health properties and healing side. Well, as they say, what's for you won't go by you and that journey was not to be.

However a journey of a much greater kind was in store and Stuart definitely had his part to play in it. To hear about healing from Stuart came as no big shock to me. After all my mother had spoken openly on the subject. Indeed one time I got my palms read by a lovely old lady who told me that I had healing in my hands, but she also told me that once I opened an ancestral door I must be prepared to pay the piper. I did not have the foggiest idea what she was talking about until some years later.

After Stuart left I started teaching Tai-Chi in September of that same year, ten years after I first started studying it. I taught it only to small groups of people at first and they received amazing benefits. A lot of them noticed that their health was improving. One of my students later put it like this: 'Tai-Chi has made a big change in my life. I have not had a single flu in four years. I am certainly more confident and balanced in how I perceive people and events.'

At this time too a lot of people were telling me I had healing qualities, and that I would develop them in time. Priests, nuns, religious and non-religious people, spiritual teachers and martial arts instructor, in fact all classes of people from over the world said pretty much the same thing. This, however, did not really come as a big a surprise to me, as by now I was occasionally dabbling

Peter, Hugh, Daniel and myself

with energy and works of that nature: such as making objects hot and cold to touch or making them heavy or light by using my mind.

Many a time my three boys and I would have good fun with these experiments when Grace was away shopping. It was a bit like hypnosis. Looking back at it now it seems to me that this was my training for the future. This sort of thing did not go on for too long _ at least not once I realised that I did not get this energy or mind-power for bending spoons and stopping watches. Not that I have anything against these things, if that's what people want to do, but I knew somehow that there was something else behind this unusual energy.

Sometimes I would try my hand at healing on family members. I remember once reading an article in a Kung Fu magazine about this Qi-Gong doctor called Caho Yuanfang of the Sui Dynasty around 581 AD. He could heal people just by the power of his mind, by allowing his own Chi or energy to emanate from the centre of his hands without even touching the people. It was said that when someone had mastered the art of Qi-Gong they were able to release, through their hands, a sort of vital energy, which could heal others. So I tried this on my aunt in our living room in July 1993 and both she and I were surprised at the results. She described it afterwards: 'I can get a strong feeling of heat off your hands and the room is full of tranquillity and peace.' She felt great relief from her pain. This was the end of my doing tricks with my mind as I had now discovered different talents. I could help people to relax and ease their pain and discomfort by the power of my mind. This is all a bit like growing up: for instance, you might spend a while doing art and later on go on to write poetry and so on until you find what's right for you. This is how we develop.

Another time I was at the Mary from Dungloe festival giving it all to the music of the band "Goats Don't Shave". A few feet away from me a lady fell. My sister-in-law who was with me ask me to help her – what happened then was most peculiar. The lady could feel movement in her ankle and I instantly knew she had twisted all the ligaments in her ankle, all before I even touched her. She got a bit upset on account of this, and immediately I put my hands on her shoulder and everything was fine again. She sort of dozed off for those few minutes that I was with her. Anyway, to cut a long story short, I did a healing on her and went back to the concert. That was fine and I thought no more about it. Before the concert was over the lady came and thanked me. I'll never forget her exact words: 'Thanks very much' she said, 'whoever you are', indeed I never forgot her either, although I never laid eyes on her from that day to this. The whole experience was certainly an eye-opener for me and gave me the confidence to continue with the healing.

There were many times, when people spotted something about me, that would perhaps make me stand out a little in a crowd, although I never considered myself any different from anyone else.

5

All the Big Boys

Once I was at a Ju-Jitsu seminar in Dublin given by Professor Richard Morris, Head of Ju-Jitsu International.

Yes, I met all the big boys – or so I thought. Professor Morris was a lovely man, with hypnotic, psychic and healing qualities himself. From the very first moment we met he showed a strong interest in me and in my talents. He asked me to do a healing on one of his students the day before I went home. Later on he told me that before I started the healing my guide was made known to him. He could see this old man with a white beard working with me as I performed the healing on his students. He also told me that I did not get my energy for martial purposes. He put it like this: 'Charlie, the bubble is about to burst!' And burst it did. Nothing could have prepared me for what was about to happen, although everything was staring me in the face. I didn't manage to put the whole picture together until May 1994. That year would change my life forever. Thankfully it has not changed me as a person, and thankfully my family could handle it.

By the early 1990s I was getting more and more involved in the health side of things and moving further away from the martial side. By this time I was practising and teaching Tai-Chi here and there, doing the odd healing from time to time. Some days the drive would be blocked with cars of clients coming from different parts of the county, having heard about me by word of mouth.

At this time my good friend Tom Hodgins asked me to give a two-day lecture and workshop on Tai-Chi and Qi-Gong in Maynooth University, Co. Kildare. This was the first of many workshops.

The minute I got the offer the name rang a bell with me, for two reasons. Firstly, my sister Mary went to college there. I also knew from my mother's stories, that my granduncle, Dr Michael O' Donnell, was Professor of Moral Theology there in the past. Our family had a high regard for Maynooth. When my father heard that I was to teach there, he was ever so pleased. On the morning I left for Maynooth he told me not to forget to say a prayer for Dr Michael, and to thank him for helping me to get to teach in one of the finest universities in Ireland.

Well, this message went in one ear and out the other until I got to the end of the second day of the workshop. It had all gone like clockwork: I was teaching brilliantly a group of strangers without a flutter. My friend Tom remarked, 'This is great where the hell is it coming from?'

I replied, 'I don't know but I hope it keeps on coming until I get out of here.'

For my part I could not understand at all the different vibes in the college. There were mixed feelings: a feeling of tranquillity in the place where I was teaching and a feeling of despair and

Ju–Jitsu seminar in Maynooth, Co. Kildare.

Teaching Taiji in Maynooth University, Co. Kildare

hopelessness in the other buildings. Perhaps this was because of my first impressions. When I first arrived in Maynooth I met an old monsignor. When I told him that I was there to teach Tai-Chi and things of a spiritual nature, he was very angry and remarked that this was the occult or something of that sort. I thought him a sad and lonely man, with a very closed mind and I was not going to be told by a clergyman what I could and could not teach.

This may come as something of a surprise to the reader since after all I had come from a religious background. But even at an early age, priests and clergy seemed to me not to have the foggiest idea about true spiritual matters and a lot were scared stiff of them. I'm glad to see that things are changing and barriers are coming down every day. I also realised then, and now, that there's a big difference between religion and spirituality. So, after exchanging a few choice words with the monsignor, I made my departure and continued with the rest of the group. I must say that they were the nicest bunch of open-minded young people I ever met. One of them would play an important part in the development of the Castle and my healing abilities, His name was Enda Butler and at that time he was a student of anthropology in Maynooth University.

To the present day he remains one of my dearest friends and I owe him a great deal of gratitude.

During the workshop Enda and I struck a chord, although Enda did not take in a word of what I was teaching that day. He said afterwards he was fascinated by my aura, or magnetic field around my body. Nowadays they have cameras that can photograph this energy field around the body. Although I never got such a photo taken, I did have aura readings done, and they were good fun.

Enda Butler and myself

At the end of the workshop Enda showed me around the college because at about five o'clock I had this terrible urge to see the picture of my granduncle Dr Michael, whom my father had mentioned to me before I left for Maynooth.

Enda and I spent such a long time looking around dormitories for my uncle's portrait that I almost missed my bus home. Then at last I saw this picture far up in the top dormitory, and recognized the man as being somewhat like myself. I had to look twice at the portrait to make sure that it was the right person, although I could see the family resemblance immediately. Enda could see it too. Enda gave me a few minutes to get my head around things and in those few minutes everything made sense. It was as if the picture spoke to me although I heard nobody physically speak to me. Three times I intuitively heard the message: 'Go home and open the Castle.'

'Go home and open my house and do my work.' That work, I later understood, was healing.

At that moment you could have knocked me down with a feather but when Enda came back and I told him what had happened he did not seem one bit surprised. It was as if he knew that this was going to happen. But even then I couldn't put things together. It was not until Enda came to visit me in my home in Donegal that everything fell into place.

The Castle after renovations 1994

Enda wrote me a humble letter asking me to teach him Tai-Chi as he was going to use it for part of his thesis. Naturally I agreed and when Enda arrived in Donegal a month later everything my mother had told me as a young boy seemed to make sense at last. However before Enda got there I had to face the challenging task of breaking the news to my family that I was going to open the Castle.

The Castle is an imposing, comfortable, two-storey house set back from the road. It was built on a commanding site with an amazing view of the Bluestack Mountains on one side and of Errigal on the other. It originally had tennis lawns and gardens to the front. Everyone in the area knew the Castle, my great-grandparents' house and the home of the late Dr Michael. They also knew the stories that went with it, mostly local ghost stories. Everyone was a little curious about this big two-storey house that had been closed for the previous thirty-odd years.

I too was terrified of going to the Castle when I was a young child. As I grew older from time to time when things got on top of me I would find refuge there and in the woods close by.

When I came back from Maynooth refreshed after a great workshop I couldn't wait to go over to the Castle. I didn't tell anyone in the house where I was going, just made the excuse that I was going to see a neighbour. I ran across the fields as I felt there was something calling me – the spirits of the house, the inner voices or intuitive messages in my head, I wasn't quite sure. As I stood at the bottom of the steps of the Castle, I heard this inner voice again telling me not to be afraid, and to take back what was rightfully mine. At that time I thought this meant the building but it was made very clear to me later on that the inner voice was not talking about the building but about the gift of healing that had lain dormant for years until the right time came, just as the house had waited for the right time.

I really enjoyed that morning at the Castle and I didn't want to go home, as I didn't know how I was going to tell my wife and family that I was going to open up the Castle and do healings in it. They thought I was losing my marbles this time for sure. My wife Grace on RTE's Nationwide TV programme used that very phrase openly some years later. Grace always speaks her mind, but then again Grace speaks for the public and she has always been a great strength and inspiration to me. But in the beginning she didn't understand – and who would blame her? She wasn't happy with my opening the Castle. I felt that this was a test; there would be more to come, as I was to find out later.

I soldiered on and finally everything came together like one great big jigsaw. It is still being put together as I write this. I went against the wishes of all my family and wrote to the current owners, the O' Neill family. Immediately a feeling of kinship was struck up. A date was arranged for me to meet them and finally to get the key of the Castle.

In the meantime however, my guides or angels were at work. I prefer to call them guides, as I believe I had guides at this stage: there were too many happenings that could not all be coincidences. I thought a lot about what to write to the owners of the Castle. I wanted to make a good impression, in the hope they would let me rent the house. They did not know me from Adam, although they knew my family. One night as I was about to put pen to paper I had a phone call from another member of the same family. She was living here in Ireland. She told me that her sister, the owner of the Castle, was in Ireland, and would be staying for a few days, and, if I liked, I could meet her. I could not believe my luck, and once again my guides came to help me. By this time I couldn't wait to meet her and to get inside the Castle. So, the following Tuesday she and I met outside the Castle.

The Castle after it was built 1916

6

Dust and Cobwebs

The next Tuesday was a lovely May morning I remember it as if it were yesterday. I was relaxed and full of confidence. It was as if I was in control of the whole meeting. From the very beginning the owners of the Castle and I got on like a house on fire.

I told them that I intended to open up their house as a training and healing centre. I would bring people and students from all over Ireland, or indeed the world, to teach them my skills. They were, to say the least, quite excited about the whole project. This was my intention at first. But, although I did some classes and workshops there, until a few years ago, my guides had other plans for me. This was revealed to me the minute I walked inside the door of the Castle with the owners. The house was shrouded with dust and cobwebs but it had a lovely warm atmosphere about it. The energy felt heavy and dense. But I knew that this was my great grandparents' house. What was there to be afraid of?

As I entered the house I got a most welcoming 'hello', and later on, when I was healing there, my clients felt very welcome in the house. They would sometimes remark that there was something very special about the place.

That morning as I stepped into the hallway, apart from the dust and cobwebs coming at me, there were messages coming left, right and centre. Although the owners were talking about this and that, I'm afraid I was not paying any attention to them. I was being bombarded with messages and mental pictures in every corner of the house. The next powerful message I got was when I was heading up the stairs: 'You are only a guest here, but a most honoured one.' It was at that moment that I knew my stay would be short, and that somehow I was there to learn my trade as a healer.

Sarah O' Neill and I had a great time that day chatting about this and that, as if we knew each other all our lives. Before she left she gave me the key to the Castle which was very special to me.

After Sarah left I started cleaning up the place. There was a lot to clean. Although I was in the house by myself, I felt I was being watched, but in a nice sort of way. Indeed every room I went into was giving off pleasant peaceful vibes and telling me a different story. The house seemed to have a mind of its own; indeed every room seemed to have a mind of its own. I was very relaxed and after a while, it felt like walking into my own home. The spirits or energy of the house and my own guides or inner voices were like two kids playing. They too, got on like a house on fire.

I was expecting Enda to come and see me. One day I was cleaning the grass away from the doorway of the Castle, making it a little more presentable for his visit. I was truly exhausted by now, what with all the letter-writing, studying, teaching – not to mention working on my first manuscript, Tai-Chi for Everyone, being a father, and husband and running my home. I said 'How under God will I do this?' I immediately heard a voice, only this time, to my surprise, it was loud and clear, and what I might call physical. 'Put a chair in the lower room, and the rest will fall into place,' the voice said, and into place it did. I started healing upstairs at first – I was not listening to my guides – but my guides stepped in and directed me downstairs to the lower room. This was the room in which my late granduncle, Dr Michael, read Mass to the local people when he came home on holidays from Maynooth. All this time I was reading books of a more spiritual nature, rather than martial arts, and meeting a lot of spiritual and open-minded people, not to mention the spirits of the house. I was getting quite used to them by now, which made Enda' s visit less alarming.

7

An Uphill Struggle

Enda arrived at the Castle in June 1994 just a month after I met him in Maynooth. Although he was a young student he had the wisdom of a ninety-year-old man but, as he has pointed out to me many times, age has nothing to do with it. We are all far too caught up with age and the ageing process. We should not think in terms of numbers, or of years lived, but we should think of life as essence that feeds constantly from within. Enda's comment left me in deep thought and suddenly this sentence came into my head: 'Why feel old just because time passes?' There was something about these words that I will never forgot. They reminded me that we should always be young at heart and to keep our imaginations alive. I never conveyed these words to Enda as he was full of wisdom and wise sayings himself and there was something about his presence that would attract your attention. To me he was always in the centre and nothing would upset him. His calmness was remarkable. On that and other visits we became the best of friends. Apart from our doing a few Qi-Gongs there wasn't much in the way of Tai-Chi being taught. Everything from day one was as if it had been planned to get me prepared for the work that lay ahead.

The voices had stopped but the messages kept coming. I asked lots of questions on spiritual matters and the likes, and there were many Enda was able to answer. I recall one funny instance. It was after Enda and I had done some energy work – aura balancing, meditation – that my past life regressions came to the surface. I could see myself as an old man dressed in a black-and-white suit not unlike my Tai-Chi suit, but with a little more red and green woven into it. I had a white beard and a staff, a bit like the staff that goes with me on seminars. Here I could see myself in bare feet, teaching and healing in another land, perhaps eastern Asia. The whole experience lasted for the best part of an hour, with similar experiences that I wish to keep to myself. Anyway, after everything had settled down I was exhausted. I said to Enda that we had better go home because Grace would wonder where we were. I remember his reply, which has made us laugh many times since: 'We can't go home yet because Grace won't recognise you.'

Anyone who has gone through past regressions will know what I am talking about. These and similar experiences – like visiting my secret garden (the likes of which I think everyone should have), where I often went in my mind during my meditation practice_ happened nearly all the time when Enda came to visit me in the Castle in my first few years as a healer. He was sent to me as a guide, to get me ready and to help me to listen. I was slow in listening to my own spiritual guides, as one so often is– or rather, it's one thing to listen to your guides but it's another thing to act on their advice. All my life I've been fortunate enough to do both. My guides have been a great source of advice to me, in and out of the healing circle, and in everything I undertook. I'm not saying it was easy but, as they say, a little struggle is a must. Sometimes we need a helping hand. Enda, and others like him who crossed my path from time to time, were a great help, guiding me and building my confidence in what I was doing and in what I was going to do in the future.

One such person to whom I owe a great deal of thanks is a nun named Sr Monica. I did not want to have anything to do with the religious on these matters but she was different, with a truly open-minded approach to healing and spiritual matters. She suited me down to the ground. So I was blessed when Tom Hodgines advised me to go and see her, and ask for her advice on healing. Both Tom and Grace were a little concerned at the time about what was going on with me. And Tom pointed out to me that, if I had the gift of healing, Sr Monica was the one who would put me right. All of this was happening around the time I met Enda. Because of what was going on I felt compelled to go and see her, as I knew I was somehow drawn to her. I knew that there was more to this than Tai-Chi or Qi-Gong, although Tai-Chi and Qi Gong meditation had brought my gifts to the surface.

I never learned meditation from anyone; I just dabble in it. But looking back now I know that this was not the way to go about it. Sr Monica remarked, when she saw me, that I was being used, certainly, but that I was being well looked after. On my visit to Sr Monica I brought my sister Mary along, who was well versed in religious matters and would not be fooled by any Tai-Chi 'rubbish', as she might have considered it at the time. She wanted answers too, I suppose, so she would be able to break the news gently to my father and the rest of the family. Sr Monica took no more than ten minutes to see where I was coming from and what was going on with me. She turned to my sister and said, 'I wish I could buy your brother's gifts.' I then asked Sr Monica if she would like to see me meditating and she said she would. I started to meditate but my sister did not see me do this, as somehow she dozed off for that period. She herself put it down to the long journey we had had that day, but I think that perhaps my meditation was too much for her to take in, as it was no ordinary run-of-the-mill meditation.

I meditated for Sr Monica. A meditation that was later to become known as 'becoming the circle', one of the seven set practices in my second book, A Way To Healing. When I finished the meditation, which lasted about three minutes, Sr. Monica said to me, 'It does not take you long to get there and you certainly know your passport back.' What she meant was that I have the power in my mind to forget everything else and concentrate on the job in hand – the healing. I could put myself into a trance -like state at will and raise my own spirit or vibrations to allow my guides (or as she put it my angels) to work through me. This is known as attunement with spirit. Professor Morris was another man who witnessed this event, when he watched me perform a healing on one of his students.

By now it was time to say good-bye to Sr. Monica, but before our departure she asked me for a healing. Then she blessed both my sister and myself and told me to trust in the Lord, and that my granduncle was looking out for me from the next world.

One would imagine that I came back to Donegal with a swelled head after all of that, but I was much more composed than ever now. I was ready to take on the world, not to mention take over my great-grandparents' house, and to continue the work that my granduncle had started, although the healing could now reach a lot more people than in his time. I came under no umbrella or restrictions of the church like in his day. Priests in my granduncle's time were not encouraged to practise healing openly. This is why gifts like these have left the church, but no doubt they will return one day when the time is right. Every day more and more barriers are coming down; these matters are not now as controlled as they were in the past. So I was a free entity and would not answer to anyone but my higher self, and the higher forces that work with me. I would have no interference, physical or spiritual – as my so-called spirits of the Castle found out later on.

Enda visited me as often as he felt necessary and during those visits he would relay messages about the healing and about my guides. He said it was entirely up to me whether I wanted to do the healing or not. There was no problem if I did not agree to continue with the healing. He relayed this message to me when I was back in Maynooth again, just a couple of weeks before the official opening of the Castle as a healing centre.

During all this time I was keeping close contact with my good friend, Stuart Lee Marseny, now head of his own association "International Internal Arts Association". Stuart happened to be in Europe at this time so I wrote to him, and he agreed to do the official opening at the Castle. He was excited and very pleased with my progress. At that time I was also in close contact with the Derry Tai-Chi playhouse group, where I first met up with the late Danny Connors.

Danny Connors, sadly, has passed on. Although I had his book and video in the early 1980s, long before I met him, it was great to meet him in person, and get his autograph on my copy of his book.

Tai-Chi playhouse group Derry,

Danny is a huge loss to the Tai-Chi world, but I still have memories of him. One of them I will share with you now.

When we met we struck a chord, not in the usual way but in a funny old way, I suppose. When I told Danny that I was doing healing, he laughed and said, 'I hope you heal more than you kill.' I had so much energy in me at that time that the only way I could express it was through the old form of Fajine Tai-Chi, which is a very fast martial form of Tai-Chi. I still had a lot of anger to let go of, and in a nice and gentle way Danny saw this in me. I was no stranger to the Tai-Chi playhouse group in Derry, and when the members heard that I was opening a training and healing centre, naturally they gave me all the support I needed. Fate was once again on my side. It so happened that one of the world's Tai-Chi masters, When Whui from China, was giving a workshop in Derry around this time. Charlie Morrison of the Derry playhouse told me that she would appear as a special guest on the opening day of the Castle. I was over the moon, as it seemed that my guides thought of everything. This was no coincidence; it was their very way of acknowledging the uphill struggle I had had from my early days of training. I could not believe that a Tai-Chi master was coming all the way from China, and that I would get the chance to meet her.

Charlie and his friend Cathy brought When Whui to see me at my home in Kilraine about a week before the official opening of the Castle.

The minute I laid eyes on When Whui she reminded me of my mother, as she had a nice and gentle way with her.

When Whui and myself

We went for long walks around Kilraine. We chatted about the internal arts most of the time that we were together, although she did not give much information away as I did most of the talking. She was, however, a bit surprised at the amount of information and physiological material I had on the internal arts. At this time I had assembled a huge body of information on the subject, both of the healing and combat properties of Tai-Chi and Qi-Gong, with the help of Erle Montaigue of the WTBA, to whom I had been writing for a number of years. I have to thank Erle for his help, because sometimes he would send me information free of charge. He wrote to me then, and since then some lovely letters, with great advice on the internal arts, but mostly about healing. In one of those letters he wrote these encouraging words. Charlie, the centre of your palms is warm because the Chi is coming out from Laugone point in the centre of your palm; this is good. Sometimes so much heat is generated that it leaves the fingers colder. This is normal and means that you are probably getting it.'

He also wrote the foreword that follows below: '

Foreword

by Erle Montaigue (Master Degree China) WTBA.

I have the pleasure of writing the foreword for Charlie's, book. He has done a wonderful job of putting into plain English a very difficult subject so that everyone can understand what this healing/martial art is all about.

Tai-Chi for Everyone is for everyone, beginner or advanced student. There is much in there that will interest anyone who has ever wanted to know more about this great art than just a few slow movements.

Erle.

Erle and myself doing some push hands in 2005

So it was no wonder that I could converse easily with When Whui on these matters. She never mentioned the healing and I never brought it up again. There were so many other things to talk about and look at.

She was really taken with Kilraine, the peacefulness and beauty of the whole countryside. Today, many of my clients still are. I remember well one American couple who remarked when they arrived that they could almost taste the air here.

Cathy and Charlie, of the Tai-Chi playhouse in Derry, came to see me a few times before the official opening. We had a wonderful time exchanging different ideas on Tai-Chi and the healing properties of Qi-Gong. They were really impressed by the whole idea of the training and healing centre in Kilraine and the Castle itself, and this is how they described it in their letter of August 1994: 'The Castle is most definitely 'situated in an area of Donegal which is surrounded by magnificent scenery, which in itself will act as a magnet for many visitors who will come here."

It seemed now that everything was working according to plan and coming together like clockwork. Enda and Stuart arrived the night before the opening. That was a great meeting for the three of us, as we all seemed to have had a part to play in putting the whole jigsaw together. Stuart was very pleased to see me and was totally overwhelmed by the transformation of the Castle. He too contributed a foreword for my book *Tai-Chi For Everyone*

As regards the Castle he also reminded me of these words of inspiration, which I think say it all. 'There is nothing so powerful in all the world as an idea whose time has come.' Never was there a truer saying.

Foreword by Stuart Lee Marseny

I am indeed pleased to have been asked to write this foreword for *Tai-Chi for Everyone*, because Tai-Chi is for everyone, and with this easy-to-understand guide/manual it has indeed been made available to everyone.

My association with Charles Shovlin has been relatively brief, but that association has borne fruit incredibly quickly. When I first met Charles it was as a the result of a letter which was posted from Ireland to my home in Australia, and then was sent on to me, eventually finding me in Waterford in the south of Ireland, where I was holidaying with my wife and family at the time. The letter was enquiring as to the possibility of my conducting a lecture and workshop in Kilraine Co. Donegal. I rang Charles and immediate kinship was struck up. I, of course, conducted the workshop /lecture and this took place in July 1993.

I travel throughout the world teaching and lecturing on all aspects of the inner arts Tai-Chi Qi-Gong, but rarely have I had such an eager and talented student as Charles. His retention of the information I passed to him was quite incredible, and his dedication to the training with me while I was staying at his home, and after I left, using the videos and written material that I supplied to him, was absolute. The result of that dedication brings me back once again to Co. Donegal to open the

Castle centre, to once again conduct a workshop and to write the foreword to this excellent work.

The training we did together and the information that was passed to Charles allowed him to cure a long-standing illness in himself, and awakened in him a long dormant family trait of healing when in need.

Even the Castle Training and Healing Centre was originally built in 1916 as a family home by a member of Charles's family, Dr Michael O' Donnell himself a noted healer. This all points to the success of this excellent work and the Castle, and I am pleased and proud to have the Castle associated with many similar centres throughout the world, including Gunneabh in Australia, La Maison Da Tao – which means the house of the way – in France, and the Heyokah Centre in Wales, as well as others in Sweden, Russia, Scotland and Norway, currently under construction.

The International Internal Arts Association, of which Mr Shovlin is the Irish representative and coordinator, is committed to fostering the development of the area of Tai-Chi and Qi-Gong and this book can only help enormously in this work.

Stuart Lee Marseny.

Head of the International Internal Arts Association

Although Stuart retired early that night, as he had a busy two days ahead of him, Enda and myself chatted well into the night about how much we had learned in spiritual matters in just a few short months, and how this whole project had come together so quickly. The Castle was jumping with a delightful energy that night. My whole family as well as friends and neighbours were up half the night making sandwiches for the next day.

The next day was the official opening day, a day that changed my life forever. It was truly a wonderful day with some magnificent displays of Tai-Chi and Qi-Gong. There was a very gentle form of Tai-Chi performed by When Whui and the Derry playhouse group.

Stuart & myself at The Official Opening

There was a very powerful display of Fajin, the old fast energetic form of Tai-Chi, performed magnificently by Stuart and his student Peter also from Australia.

The Derry Tai-Chi Playhouse Group

This made me think to myself that we had the best of both worlds here.

We had the perfect balance of Yin and Yang – total harmony with our surroundings and with the people who were there on that morning.

It is a morning I remember vividly. I stood there on the balcony of the Castle looking down at the performances of all the different kinds of martial arts. There were people there from all over the world doing their own thing. I must say that the whole experience reminded me of the film Enter the Dragon. I thought I had come a long way from the time I was thumping my hands into hot sand in my own imaginary martial arts world as a boy of fifteen back in the 1970s.

There was more to come, and it was not martial arts or even Tai-Chi. I was in that house morning, noon and night, developing my gift of healing. Even on the Sunday evening, the

Grace, myself, Sarah O' Neill and When Whui

second day after the opening, I had about nine healings. I never even got to say goodbye to half the visitors and friends who had come to the launch, but I know that they all enjoyed their time in Kilraine and at the Castle. This is one response to the events of that wonderful day that got me started: 'On behalf of our group, I would like to thank you all for a wonderful weekend of education and friendship. We stopped off in a pub on our way back, and I must say that the comments of our people were extremely complimentary about you all. In fact there was much sadness about leaving Kilraine. It was truly an international gathering of our countrymen and women and friends from all over the world, a unique occasion. Kilraine was the appropriate place for us all to meet, and we look forward to the future of the Castle with great confidence.

8

Between Worlds

That first year I must have seen up to a thousand clients and the next year as many not to mention doing workshops and lectures and running regular classes on Tai-Chi and Qi-Gong. People were hearing about me mostly by word of mouth, which I find more positive and more honest than advertising. In the beginning I never really advertised my work, apart from doing an interview on Highland Radio on the Shaun Doherty Show, and doing the odd interview over the phone about the opening of the Castle, which was featured in a lot of news papers at that time. The media were no strangers to me because of my martial arts days. I somehow knew that they would catch up with me at some time, and that they would also play their part in the development of my work.

You cannot see thousands of people in a rural area like Kilraine without the media getting wind of it. Because of my martial arts background they often printed articles for me in the sport section. Once, however, a local paper told me that I was a man before my time and they sent me packing. Most of the time they would listen to me and take what I had to offer.

Indeed, one time I had the good fortune of attending a Tai-Chi workshop in Derry which was televised by the BBC television nationwide network, so I was well used to the media. There was more to come, but at that time I still did not want to advertise – particularly not this story as I thought it might turn into a circus act. But the media were starting to get hold of the story of the Castle and me. A friend of mine, Anna, who wrote for a Belfast paper, put it like this.

Anne Marie McFaul meets a man who has discovered his healing powers.

CARRYING ON THE ANCIENT TRADITION OF HEALING

After that story got out and about, things really took off. I now started seeing people not only from Donegal and Ireland but from all over Northern Ireland, England and Scotland as well. People heard about me mostly through word of mouth. Some, however, had seen the news paper reports and came, and they told others. Sufferers with all kinds of illness and ailments were calling at the Castle to seek a cure, or at least relief from their pain. I just couldn't believe it: after all, up to a few months ago this place was a derelict building, and now people were coming from far and wide to see me - just as my mother had predicted many years before that. I was seeing people with all kinds of illness: arthritis, muscular pain, shoulder pain, leg pain, Among the most common visitors were people with back pain and bad backs.

Clients were coming from everywhere and I was doing my best to see them. I was also conducting healing over the phone and sending out absent healing letters. Absent healing or distance healing, as it is sometimes called, is the ability to increase the electro-magnetic field of a client's energy pattern to awaken the body intelligence, to neutralise and re-direct blocked energy pathways and patterns. The idea is to bring about harmony and well-being without physical contact or without having to be there at all. This might sound somewhat magical. To put it simply, all you do is project your own energy intention or pray to another person. Visualisation skill's intention is thought; thought is energy – it's as simple as that.

I remember one night I was asked to give absent healing over the phone to a lady in London. I am sure this sounds strange but in the beginning I did not touch my clients so I felt I could do healing from a distance. This particular healing, however, was very strange indeed. As I was giving the healing I got a mental picture of a street. I could say for sure that it was in London. That night alone I did about five healings in the same street and they were very powerful indeed. I had never done anything like it. I still do absent healing over the phone, but that night was special. It made me believe more in the power of the mind, and how we can connect to like minds, to help each other. I strongly believe that people should be taught to expand their minds, as a little day-dreaming never harmed anyone.

I was really flat out now with healing, and in all that time Enda would come and go and recharge my batteries, He would give me some extra knowledge on healing, and on spiritual matters. Enda was the main player in the development of the Castle. Stuart came and went; so did When Whui and the others. I lost contact with them shortly after the opening because I didn't seem to have the time. I was simply run off my feet by now, running back and forward between worlds: my home and the Castle, which was now becoming a second home for me. I spent a good part of my time there, and it became a place of peace and tranquillity for the sick, lonely and broken spirits who came to me. Healing took over my life for the next three to four years.

In the beginning I intended to open up the Castle as a training and healing centre, and to bring many alternative treatments together under one roof: treatments such as hypnotherapy, ki massage, reflexology, Tai-Chi and Qi-Gong and aromatherapy. The world's leading aromatherapist, Christine Westwood from England, and Peter Shield, the Belfast Reiki Master Teacher, did workshops there in the beginning. This made me realise that there was definitely a force at work here beyond this world. Up until a few months before the place had not even been heard of, and now there were masters from all over the world coming to teach in this great house of past learning. But my plan worked only for a short period as somehow my guides and the spirits of the house had other intentions. My own training and healing was much more important, so eventually all the other therapists moved on, and I was running the show on my own.

In the beginning, most, if not all, of my clients were coming to me for relief from bad backs, arthritis and pains of one kind or another. I knew intuitively that they were also coming to me on a spiritual level and that the healing was an inner healing, not just working with physical problems. My guides, early on in my training, made this known to me. Although sometimes we think of sickness as a curse, this is not so; this is the way that we are given to further evolve spiritually and come to full spiritual awareness.

Although I was run off my feet, I would be excited when a person would leave their pain behind them. I remember a girl coming to see me shortly after I opened the Castle. She had severe pain in her foot. I did a healing on her, which lasted about thirty minutes. That is the usual length of my sessions although some may last longer, depending on the circumstances. Although she was totally relaxed during the healing, she remarked afterwards that she was still the same, and still had the pain. I told her to be patient and wait to see what happened within the next few days. Three days later I was in the Castle, just pottering around, when the phone rang. It was the girl's mother on the line, and I clearly recalled the conversation. The mother asked, 'What did you do to my daughter?' I thought, "O my God," and replied, 'I did nothing.' I reassured her that I didn't lay hands on any of my clients. (But that was to change too, as life is all about change). She said, 'You must have done something because my daughter has not a pain nor an ache.' When I put the phone down, I ran to the top of the stairs with sheer delight, as if I had just won the lotto, but it was far better than any lotto, then or ever since.

I remember also in my early days of healing that a gentleman came to see me from Glasgow with a very painful back. He was so bad that he walked with a limp. I did a healing on him and he got a lot of relief in those first few moments. It was so relaxing for him that he almost fell asleep. This happens quite a lot when I do my healings. After the healing was over he felt much better and said, 'Maybe I won't need this stick after all.' I couldn't get over the fancy walking-stick he had. It was a really nice one that folded up neatly like one of my wife's umbrellas It happened that he never really needed that fancy stick. I am sure it is still in the back of his car. Although he did not get rid of all his pain in that first visit he came back several times to see me since and thankfully he has never looked back. This story has a twist to it. He had bought the walking-stick in a particular shop, and the shop owner's daughter was suffering at the time from severe arthritis. She happened to ask him one day, 'How come you're not using your stick? In fact, how come you're walking so well? He told her about the healing and myself. She and her husband came to see me the following summer, as she was crippled with arthritis. She got great relief and never looked back. This is a letter from her husband:

> Dear Charles
>
> Thank you for the time spent with my wife and myself and for the relaxation she got after our visit. My wife's back has been great since talking to you, and we would both like to thank you for sharing your gift with us, and the changes it has made to our lives. Even the children notice the difference.
>
> Yours sincerely
>
> R. Watson

This was a wonderful moment for myself as indeed all healings are, when clients leave their pain behind them. It's the greatest joy in the world for me and makes everything worthwhile. There were many moments like this which were full of excitement, and which would take up a book of their own.

9

Learning the Trade

The other great excitement I got was when my guides would work through me, both in healing and meditation. Although I did not see them, I could certainly sense them, and feel their energy entering and leaving. They greeted me as I started my day's work, the same as if I were greeted entering my best friend's house. These inward conversations I had with my guides, during and after healings, would sometimes have a sense of humour about them. They kept reminding me that a person with a good sense of humour was truly blessed, and that we don't lose our personality just because we lose our physical body. In other words, the mind never dies. The mind has many levels, and the soul is just one of these. The soul has infinite energies, and all energies have different levels. In spiritual matters everyone develops in their own time, and in many lifetimes. The sum total of what you have been, good or bad, is what you are now. This makes the subject of past lives complicated. Indeed, it is better left alone, because genetic memories become mixed up with our own mind memories of those of our ancestors. We all have to live our lives while paying for our ancestors' actions, and the damage that they have done to their psyche.

All these conversations kept me going when I had busy days, and the results kept on coming. The healings were getting more powerful, and more and more clients were coming from all over the country and Europe as well. Because of that, more and more guides wanted to use me in healing. There was so much ancestral energy about the Castle that I felt very much at home there. Sometimes, however, it would interfere with the healing energy, and my own energy. Even though the Castle was empty, apart from my clients and myself, to me it seemed almost full most of the time. There was something always going on there: some plan of action, preparing for healing or messages coming and going. Sometimes this made it hard for me to concentrate.

Every room seemed to have a dimension of its own, which had a different purpose. I called each room a different name to suit the spiritual work that was going on there. This reminded me of my secret garden that I saw early in my meditations, long before this all happened. For instance I had a room of learning books and teachings where I got a lot of ideas and inspiration for writing and for learning. There was a room of change where messages would be relayed of the past, present, and future. Here I was reminded of how unimportant the future is, as it's the present that counts, and also that we should not dwell in the past. I was reminded that healing was priceless, and that I should never crave for money, or any material thing. So, from day one, there was no fee for healing. The rest room was where I often meditated, and I stayed there one night till morning and slept like a baby. I woke up totally refreshed and charged to go into the last room, the healing room. This was a private room.

What went on there as regards the healing, was between me and my clients, and their God, whatever they perceived their God to be.

I recall one instance in the healing room, of not so nice a nature. I was giving a healing to a lady, and her friend insisted on coming in without the lady's consent. I asked her to remain outside. She went out but kept banging on the door, quite hard. I knew from the noise she was making that she wasn't going to leave. I realised that no matter what we do in life we must be in control, so I took one great breath and shouted to her, at the top of my voice, to leave. Immediately the knocking stopped.

So every room had, if you like, a mind of its own, or an energy of its own, which had to be dealt with, and given some attention. A spiritualist remarked one time, when she came to visit me at the Castle, that I should have helped to deal with ancestral, and other, energies in the Castle.

I thank my ancestors for getting me started, and for guiding me along in the beginning, but I realised that I was a separate entity, with my own spiritual helpers. In the beginning, these helpers worked through my ancestral energies – through Dr Michael – so that I would be more comfortable with the whole idea. Although they were telling me of spiritual values, sometimes the whole picture would appear quite confusing to me. Indeed, I remember once reminding them that I thought it was no good for their own spiritual journey to be hanging around for the party, i.e. the healing. However, they would quickly remind me in their own humorous way that this was their journey too, and it was far from over. They said they were happy that I was coming to the realisation of it all. I didn't quite understand the whole picture yet, but somehow I knew that they would share their understanding with me, at a later date, when the time was right.

Apart from my ancestral energies, there were other energies in the Castle that I did not understand or accept. I realised that my ancestral energies were part of this whole plan, and had more of a right to be here than myself. I also knew that I was a separate entity, with my own personal guides working with me, so I made a decision that no other entity would interfere with the healing, except I invited them on board. This worked for a long time but eventually everyone wanted a piece of the energy, and a piece of the action. As well as clients now coming in their droves, spirits were popping up out of the woodwork. The Castle was becoming like a surgical unit because spirit operations, (as I saw it), were taking place so frequently.

I remember one time, when I was giving a healing to a young man with a very stiff and painful back, there was present a whole team of doctors, or what looked like doctors. I could see everything in my mind's eye, as quite often mental pictures were relayed to me. Very often too, I could sense the energies of the guides. These doctors seemed to be performing some kind of operation on this man, although he did not feel a thing, as he was almost asleep. During the healing I was asked to move away from my client. As I did, he literally rolled over on his side and my team of healers went to work on him. This took about fifteen minutes. When all was over, the team of spiritual doctors, that was teaching me new skills in relation to back trouble and arthritis, thanked me and left. Then the man got up and walked around the room freely without a single pain or ache, and his back was as straight as a pin. He was, to say the least, quite surprised, and asked me how I did it. I replied that it was not important how I did it, that what was important was that he could get back to work again and look after his family.

There were many instances of this kind of healing in my first three years as an apprentice healer. My guides quite often pointed out to me that I was only an apprentice healer. They said I didn't get these abilities handed to me on a plate, although I had been picked out because I suited the task, because I had the energy and commitment, and most of all, I had the compassion to be a healer. These are the three things you need to have as a healer: you need the energy to keep you going, commitment to be there for your clients, and, most of all, you need the compassion to see and honour the spirit that dwells within each client.

Every now and again a new group of spiritual healers would work through me. I would be learning new ways of dealing with the sick, through the power of my mind, for instance, with visualisation techniques. I would visualise unravelling bad backs, arthritic joints, twisted and torn ligaments, with the power of my mind, and this reminded me of unravelling the ropes we used in the harvest time. I used a different visualisation technique when dealing with arthritis of the joints. I would see in my mind's eye the calcium carbonate molecules melting down, breaking away, and freeing the client's joints. I also got strong images of a person's health or energy field, seeing auras and charkas, and learning to balance these energy channels. I never tried to diagnose anyone, as I think this is a practice that healers should avoid.

Every now and then there would be some kind of test to overcome, to test the openness of my mind, and my commitment as a healer. There seemed to be no test for compassion; perhaps that was all taken care off back in the early 1970s when I looked after my mother. Every now and then new guides would come my way. I recall one very strange incident. Even today my family talk about it, as it was a very strange experience for us all.

One evening, late in the summer of 1995, we were all sitting at home having our tea. Two men arrived at our door; they could only be described as two monks. They were very tall men, well over six feet tall. They were dressed in poor clothes and wore sandals, and they both carried a staff. My boys innocently remarked that they would remind you of Jesus, and one of his apostles. When they arrived they said that they were looking for a healer, and they were guided to my house. My good wife Grace looked at me, and, without any hesitation, she invited them into our home to share our evening meal. That particular evening we didn't have a lot in for tea, but, whatever we had, we shared it with the two strangers and they enjoyed it.

After tea I made my way across the fields to the Castle, as I always had healings in the evening. Shortly afterwards one of the men, whose name I forget, also made his way over to the Castle. We talked for some time, and during the conversation the man relayed messages to me about the healing and the work I was doing. He told me to meditate and pray for mankind. He said that this was a much bigger picture than I thought. He was referring to the Castle and what it stood for. Then he chanted and his chants were breathtaking. I never heard anything like it before or since. After the chanting was over he asked me for a healing. Just as I was entering the healing room, he stopped me and said to wait: 'They are preparing the room for us.' In a little while we went into the room and I gave him a healing. During the healing more messages were relayed to me, not so much regarding the healing this time – more about my writings and teachings. Not so much the Tai-Chi either. The main message was that I was to teach people to connect, to connect to their essence. It wasn't until later, much later, that I understood these messages. When we finished he thanked me. Then the other man arrived over to the Castle after entertaining my family with his music. We chatted for a while until it was time for them to go. When I asked the man who had spent most time with me where they were going, his answer was this, 'We'll just follow the light.' I thought to myself for a moment, it's a pity we can't all do that. Life would be so much easier, would it not?

10

Burned Out

After the men left I got a message, to phone over to my house, and to tell Grace to put some money in an envelope and give it to the two strangers. I was told in the message that what we give out comes back tenfold, as this is the law of the universe, and nothing, or no one, can change it. This message has stood to me to this very day and the money I gave to those men that evening has certainly come back tenfold. Although I never charged for a healing, as I think it's something that you should not put a price on, I've been rewarded ten times over for my efforts, with gifts of one kind or another. Even this computer, on which I am writing, was given to me as a gift for healing. Through all the good times, and all the excitement, there were tests along the way. I was reminded many times by my guides that I was an apprentice healer. Naturally enough, as for any apprentice I supposed, there would be some final test to undergo, so that I could evolve into the different fields of healing. At this time I was moving into the emotional side of healing.

From the very beginning I had refused to see clients who suffered from mental problems, for example schizophrenia, as

I realised early on in my practice that I would not be strong enough to deal with this kind of energy and that this was definitely not my field. But now and again we are tested, and sometimes these tests can come when we least expect them. This certainly was my own case, just when everything was going so well. I was burning the candle at both ends, taking on too much and forgetting about no one but myself, with the result that my own channels became blocked, stagnated, disconnected and confused. I was not coping with the extra flow of energy that my body was receiving. I became a little burned out without even noticing it. After all, I had done so much, and had seen so many clients in such a very short period. I suppose it was no wonder that when the biggest test of all came, I was not expecting it. That was in 1997 and it nearly made me give up the Castle and healing forever.

In 1997 channels were opening everywhere. I was writing, teaching and healing, but I was not connected, nor in control. At the time it was a nightmare. I lost all confidence in my guides, and myself as a healer. Although I had the passport, I was not using it. In other words, I was not connected. As my friend Enda pointed out to me, 'It's one thing knowing your guides, but it's another thing becoming totally dependent on them.' I had somehow become too dependent on sources outside myself. Basically, I had forgotten to connect to my own internal power. What really happened to me was that I was under the illusion that there were three things at work here: myself, my guides, and the source, or essence, or God. The result was that the channel and the messages got more confusing. In spite of everything the healings went fine, even though my emotions were scattered, because I was not connected to the essence. I later found out that there are not three parties involved in healing: there is only the source, essence, or God. However at that time I had no peace of mind, day or night. Everything seemed to get on top of me and there was a time when I could not answer the phone.

Things got so bad and confusing that I lost all my confidence as a person, not to mention as a healer. Enda knew what was going on but could not interfere, as this was not his path. I had to go this one alone. In desperation I phoned Sr Monica, and she said that she could not help me. This was my 'calling card', as she put it, but she said she had every belief that I would somehow come through this, and would be much stronger on account of it. She was right of course, but I could not see the bigger picture then. Erle Montaigue of the WTBA wrote to me at this time, as he felt that I was going through a bad patch, even though he was thousands of miles away in Australia. He too felt that I would get through it and go on to greater things. He was right; but at the time none of this seemed to be any great help to me. Clients just kept on coming, with their burden of emotional pain, and I was taking all of it on board.

Around the same time, another strange channel opened up. This I was to learn later was automatic writing. Automatic writing is, simply, writing in a relaxed state of mind anything that comes into your head, even if it seems confused or mixed up. This confusion, I was told by my guides, has to do with different channel frequencies and vibrations. These imprints or messages have to pass other dimensions and frequencies, to reach the frequency of the mind into which they can land. In my case, in spite of all the confusion at the time, these messages seemed to be in order. It was within this channel of automatic writing that I put together my second book, A Way To Healing. I wrote it to take the myth out of healing, so that it would not be kept within boundaries by putting labels on it. My guides told me that healing has no boundaries, only those we put on it ourselves. I finished the manuscript on the 8th of October 1998, the fourth anniversary of the opening of the Castle.

Near the end of 1997, things came to a head. By now, all this was affecting, not alone myself, but my family and home. Even my Tai-Chi students noticed that I was not my usual self, and advised me to stop teaching and healing. I took their advice about the Tai-Chi, but continued with the healing. I had no peace of mind, day or night; although anyone who was coming to me was coming to receive peace of mind. But the healings I did at this time were the most powerful I ever did, and had great results. All of this got me thinking. I realised I could stop my agony in the morning. All I had to do was to give up the healing. But I said to myself, 'I'm dammed if I'll do that after coming through all this.' On New Year's Night, 1998, I decided to go over to the Castle, to find out what was being asked of me. I was sick and tired of it all, and didn't care any more. Until that night I was still under the illusion that there were three parties involved in healing. That night would change my way of thinking about healing for ever.

It was one of the worst nights I can remember. It was blowing a strong gale, with some of the worst rain I can ever remember being out in. I could not feel a thing, as my temper was up. It reminded me of when I would come over there full of rage as a young boy, back in the seventies. This time my anger was more powerful and all over the place, fuelled by the power of my mind. It was a good job it was late at night, because what I said that night wasn't fit for anyone's ears. In my rage I forgot to bring the key of the Castle with me, and that made me even angrier. I let my rage out on the wall of the building, and on the spirits that were looking on at me from afar. Eventually, I ran out of steam and everything settled down, and my rage left me. For the first time in a long while, I felt peaceful and calm. Because of this tranquil and calm mind, inspiration came to me again great inspirations come in moments of peace and tranquillity. I felt my guides and the spirit of the house surround me. I also felt that I did not have to depend on them. It was all right to ask for help, but the only place to find true help is within. My intuitions and inspirations opened up to a higher level. I was reminded that I had become too dependent on Enda, Sr Monica and others. Certainly they could be there as my friends, and certainly they had their parts to play in bringing all this together. But I was reminded that the same energy or spirit that is in Enda, Sr. Monica, Stuart, Erle and in everyone else, including myself, works through us all. Some of us call it God, but it does not matter what you call it, as names are not important. It is the essence. I was reminded that we should not become too dependent on material things, and that we should stop searching outside ourselves for spirit. True spirit comes only from within. This is your higher self, or guide; a higher part of you, if you like.

This was the first time I really understood the principle of connecting to the essence, and it destroyed my illusion that there was a third party involved. I got a very strong message, which I think said it all for me: man will only find true happiness and inner peace when he stops looking outside himself to so-called sensei sifu, or masters, spiritual directors, various groups, or organisations of one kind and another. He will only find happiness when he realises that he is his own master, and that what he is searching for is already within. So that night, and the time after that, helped me to get back my peace of mind and my confidence, by letting me connect to the essence. Although I got all the different skills to work with as a healer, it is the simplicity that counts: the ability to connect to essence and experience that to which you connect. As a result of our imperfect external conditions we have, perhaps, lost our full contact with our essence. In other words, when we regard everything in the universe as being one – the essence without fear or judgement, it radiates through us, bringing health to those areas in need. Rather than considering yourself sick or not well, experience yourself as returning to optimum condition, and moving forward. The more we connect with our essence, the more we can connect and experience the essence, of that which surrounds us. It does not matter what technique you use in healing. If your heart is not in it, you will soon give up. Techniques are only there as guides to help us develop. I suppose we must start somewhere. I realised that night, and have realised ever since, that my journey started a long time ago, back in the early 1970s, as a young inquisitive boy, who went searching for something that could not be found outside myself. I realised, thirty years later, that what I was searching for was already within me.

11

Letting Go

I returned to the Castle the next day. No matter what gifts or guides worked through me, no matter what talents I had, I realised I was still only me. My gift was no different from any other gift, as all gifts are special, and everyone is equal. It was just great to be myself again. That realisation, alone, helped my confidence to improve as time went on. Although I was still seeing a lot of clients with emotional pain and suffering, it was not having the same effect on my own energy as previously, and indeed the energy in the Castle seemed to be much lighter than it had been for some time now. Once again we got on like a house on fire. Messages started to come again, but this time not as often. My own energy settled down. The shaking stopped and my concentration and confidence grew stronger daily. The healing now took on a different slant. I seemed to be working with more clients with psychological problems, although I was no psychologist. But I seemed to be able to help people in these matters, as I was able to help them let go of their emotions.

For instance, if they were angry I would advise them not to let it turn to hatred. Hatred in the heart can only lead to despair, leaving one broken-hearted and away from the sprit. Then I would tell them that anger is a good emotion, which needs to be let go, or channelled, in some positive way. I was also able to balance their energy field aura and chakras, which was another skill I was learning from the different guides that worked through me. I sometimes would tell my clients of my own anger. I would tell them to try going into a dark room and scream their heads off, or to go for long walks in the woods or on the beach, as this is a good way of letting go of emotions. I would also tell very sick or old people to use their minds if they couldn't get out of bed. Try anything, but don't hold on to anger, or don't take it out on anyone and do not take it with you - always be able to let go. It amazes me how a lot of old people would have their emotions bottled up from childhood, or from the time they were young adults. I realised how lucky I was to find a channel for my own anger.

This was the kind of healing that was done nearly every day in early 1998, though the occasional back trouble would crop up, and it was great to get the change. Things were going very smoothly for me and for the Castle. I was back teaching Tai-Chi again, and had almost finished my second manuscript "A Way To Healing". I had a lot more confidence and control in healing, teaching and writing now, than ever before. To me there wasn't a lot of difference in any of it now, as it all seemed to be woven together, as one big package, _ as the Castle's ancestral energies, my guides and myself make up one big package. What made me come to this realisation was when the time came for me to move on and leave the Castle. In the same way I was inspired to go there in May 1994, I was eventually inspired to leave the Castle and move on. I had a picture of Dr Michael in the hallway as you entered the Castle, and many a time when I walked past his picture, I would somehow get strength from it. On this particular day, in May 1998, I was walking up the hallway past his picture, and suddenly I got this message, _ as I had got the message exactly four years earlier in Maynooth telling me to open the Castle, I was now getting the message to close the Castle and move on. The message said: It's time to move on. Your time is getting short to do what you are going to do.' This message was relayed to me three times like a lot of my other messages. A lot of things in my life come in threes, such as meeting Enda, Stuart and Sr. Monica, my guides. The healing energy has an effect after three days of seeing me, although there is no guarantee. Also, this is my third and final book, and I was three years in the Castle before my final test as a healer.

I wouldn't have minded had I got this message in 1997. I would have been only too happy then to move. But I was shocked and surprised to get this message now, when I was in great form, and in control of my healing and my own emotions. I did not know what was wanted of me; after all, I felt I had been to hell and back for the healing, and for the Castle. I couldn't understand any of it. This time I did not have any anger or frustration about it; although I questioned it for a while, and it went round and round in my mind for weeks. Then, my mind was taken back to the very first day I entered these doors. The message I got that day made me realise that I was only a guest here, and that I was very lucky and blessed to be here. To share this journey with all my past ancestral energies and emotions, and people's pains and sufferings, all woven into one —a journey of realisation for us all.

I realised, like all guests, I must not abuse my welcome. I also realised that everything was part of one great picture: Dr Michael O'Donnell, the Castle, my guides and myself. But we had many different personalities. This energy, and these ancestral links, would always be with me no matter where I went. I could do my healings on the side of a mountain, it made no difference. When I closed the door of the Castle, in September 1998, I knew that I had done my last healing inside these doors. I felt sad. Then I was reminded that the Castle is only a building (a material thing) but that healing will live on for generations and that this healing would most certainly not be my last.

The Journey Home

Part Two

Strange happenings

12

The Second Phase

Well, they say that God never closes one door but he opens another. For myself this was certainly the case. He not alone opened one door, but several. A few months before I left the Castle my wife Grace dropped a hint to me about what was to be my new centre; she advised me to renovate our turf shed.

The shed was originally built as a garage, but I thought more of the turf perhaps than the car. I took Grace up on the offer, and began to use it as my new healing centre. Like everything in my life, things just fell into place. My father had built this shed in his late 80s, and I often asked him, why put cavity walls in a shed? His reply was, 'You never know what you might use it for.' How right he was. There was no way that I would let him tackle this job, at least not on his own, but once he got a trowel in his hands there was no stopping him.

So we started the work together, as I also could turn my hand to a little bit of building and rough work. I started laying out the foundation for a new turf shed, still thinking of my fire. Even though I wear T-shirts and light clothing all year round, I like a nice warm home for my family, and Grace calls me the stoker. Growing up we always had a nice warm house, and I think there is something very homely about a warm fire. So a new turf shed was first on the list, as I still had the Castle for healing.

At the time I was on the look-out for a man to help me to renovate my old turf shed, I felt my father had done enough, as he was getting on in years now. By this time the Celtic Tiger was raging in the country, and everyone was flat out, as they say. It was almost impossible to get a tradesman. However, luck was with me; I was working on a FÁS scheme where one day a friend of mine said that he would do the renovating for me. So in just three months my new place, which I called my centre, was up and running.

The centre was to give relief to the sick, lonely and broken spirits who continue to come to this very day.

It wasn't that difficult to get used to my new surroundings. When you were inside the centre it didn't look very different from the Castle. It has high ceilings and wooden floors that I deliberately designed myself, so that my guides and myself, (who were still with me, and very active), would feel comfortable in our new surroundings.

Now that everything was neutral, it wasn't long until the ancestral energies began to fade. But they were still very much with me, and in my thoughts, and occasionally they would make their presence felt. Indeed, I have a picture of Dr Michael in my healing room placed above me to remind me now and again of my roots. On the opposite wall there is a picture of my grandparents, on my father's side, to keep me grounded. Apart from those ancestral guides, who would come and oversee everything without interfering, (unless there were asked), there wasn't much excitement for nearly three years. People would turn up out of the blue, looking for a cure, or at least, relief from their pains and discomforts. Occasionally, there would be a powerful healing. I suppose every healing is powerful, given how the energy works. I still had the key of the Castle. Occasionally, I would pop

My new Healing Center 1998

over to the Castle and asked for guidance. Somehow I didn't recognize my own source of power yet, my contact with the earth and nature spirit. The Castle was starting to look a bit shabby. Even though it had been on the market for some time, I knew I wasn't quite finished there yet.

In the summer of 2001 I appeared in a magazine called *Healthy Living 2000*.

After that, I applied for a teaching job as a Tai-chi instructor and Qi-Gong therapist with a company called Tranquillity, in Letterkenny. I got the job, but that's as far as it went. Somehow it was a bit like when I joined the army; I knew when I was in the job for a while that I had done the wrong thing. I was driving home from Letterkenny but instead of going straight home I suddenly turned up at the lane for the Castle. I was out of the car before I realized where I was. I didn't have the foggiest idea what I was doing there. Somehow I knew that I had to come back to the Castle to complete some unfinished business. I went home and got the key. I was to re-open this house once again and finish my work, or so I thought.

I realised that I had to tidy up this place once again, and start teaching now in earnest, rather than healing. I suppose, healing in a different way. I'd been teaching bits and pieces of Tai-Chi and Qi Gong from there, in the previous four years, during my healing career. Somehow on this particular day I knew that I had to come out of the closet and spread this message; that, when one is connected to the earth, healing will take place automatically. It was important for me to realise at this particular time of life, that I, somehow, had a strong contact with earth, and its spirits. It was time for me to make use of this, by joining all my talents together – writing, teaching and healing – so that I could get this message across to more people. That day, I realised I had unfinished work to do. The message I got was the same I got years earlier, although I didn't make any sense out of it for a long time. 'Your time is getting short to do what you're going to do' began to make a little sense to me now.

I stood there in the lower room, as usual forgetting all about time. I was there for so long that Grace came looking for me. She is always looking out for me, and looking after my interests. I think I must have given her a shock that day because when she entered the Castle I told her to sit down, I had something to tell her. I think she thought I was going to tell her I hadn't long to live. She thought I had some bad news. Perhaps my liver was acting up on me again. When I told her I had to take over the Castle to finish my work of teaching, she was quite pleased (and relieved to hear that I was not going to die, well, at least, not yet.) Although, I had landed a great teaching job with Tranquillity, in Letterkenny, and I was to start the very next day, my guides somehow had other plans for this place, and me. Grace wasn't a bit annoyed about me turning down Tranquillity. We just seemed to laugh it off. Even the spirits of the Castle, whom I knew were there guiding both of us, seemed to laugh and joke with us as well. They seemed to be quite pleased with how this journey was going forward and entering its second phase.

Almost every day, especially on quiet days between healings, I went over to the Castle to tidy it up. This time the task was a little easier. Within the space of two weeks I had the place spick and span and ready once again for Enda's visit. He always came to visit me in the summer. Enda and I had arranged to do a one-day workshop on energy awareness and projection. We usually split up the workshop between us. This workshop went very well indeed, with Enda teaching in the morning and myself teaching in the afternoon. Grace, as usual had soup, sandwiches and tea for everyone afterwards. Sure it was like old times. Everyone who was there was impressed with the whole day, both the teaching and the hospitality they got from start to finish. The guides of the Castle were also pleased with how the guests were treated. It reminded me of how my late mother would make tea for everyone, and make everyone welcome, and that tradition is still carried on today by Grace in our own home.

That night, and the next day, Enda and his friend Violetta, (who also does Reiki like Enda), and I, went back to the Castle, to do some energy work and meditation. Enda told me that I might not be there for very long, but for now it was important to be in the Castle once again. There was a big plan for me, and I would have to be patient, and see for myself. Before he left, he invited me, and my eldest boy Hugh, to come and visit him and his parents in his home in Co. Wicklow for a few days in the New Year. He gave me a healing, as he always does, and told me I was entering the second phase of my journey. I also gave Enda and Violetta a healing before they left, and told Violetta that she had healing qualities. I told Violetta that things would fall into place, and that Enda was helping her to come to terms with it all. That is what he does: help people who are searching, and who are gifted. After they left, I continued teaching in the Castle. I taught three and four classes a week, for at least another six months. Not alone there, but all over Donegal, and indeed outside the county as well.

13

Camera-shy

Things went very smoothly for the Castle and myself during the next six to eight months. My classes were going great, everyone loved them, and I loved teaching. It gives me such a buzz to see how people change as they allow themselves to have an open mind, indeed how some of their lives changed almost overnight. So I realized that this was another kind of healing and that the Lord did indeed work in mysterious ways. Things seemed to be going quietly, even boringly, with not much happening here in the Castle, or at home either. There were still some very powerful healings, although more on an emotional level than on a physical level. I didn't really appreciate this until later on, one year later on to be precise. Then my perception of healing changed altogether, as I became more aware of my healing abilities. Once again it had taken on a different slant from that of my early days of healing.

I was being given the gift of reading people's aura or energy fields. It is a very fine way of seeing people's pasts and present, but not so much their future. I didn't really bother with that. The way I saw it; if I could help a client to stop dwelling on the past, and to live in the present, they could shape their own future, and live a fuller and happier life. This message was brought home to me when I wrote my second book, " A Way To Healing," in which one of the chapters is called 'Life is for Living'. On the physical side I couldn't see much sign of healing, as very few clients were coming to me with bad backs at that particular time, and I suppose I couldn't see the excitement in emotional healing. That didn't happen until later on.

In fact, to me, there really wasn't much happening at all, and really not that much to get excited about. That was all to change, and change it did, in a way that I would never even have dreamed of. The next year, 2002, Hugh and I went to visit Enda to do a Reiki course, as he was now a fully qualified Reiki master. I was looking forward to seeing him again. The journey started off badly, as I twisted my knee and damaged my tendon a few days before my visit, but this didn't deter us from going to Wicklow. It is a very beautiful part of the country. However, it wasn't my first time to be there, and I knew Hugh would love it. I also knew that, as always, Enda would have some guidance and messages for Hugh, and myself.

Despite my injury, we had a great weekend with Enda and his parents, who loved having us around, especially Hugh. He has this kind of energy that really livens up the place. Because I was hobbling around a lot, and couldn't do any Tai-Chi, I felt miserable. The Reiki course was wonderful. Enda seemed to pick up on my feelings, and knew that my injured knee wasn't just a physical injury. What was going on inside was manifesting itself on the outside. I believe that all injuries are signs of what is going on inside, especially knee injuries, which are a sign of a change of direction or indeed need of support. During my healing session with Enda he picked up on my feelings, and the way things were going for me in the centre. He knew I was a bit bored because I wasn't that busy. I think, it is part of my family's makeup to be busy, as my father always kept us busy.

After that healing session things changed almost instantly. It was as if someone pushed a button. We were no sooner finished and about to go home when the phone rang. It was my wife Grace. She told me RTE's Nationwide TV programme wanted to do a story about my work and me. I was totally amazed and excited, and above all, quite nervous. I said to Enda, who picked up on my nerves, 'How will I handle this?' He replied, 'Be yourself.' That's the same way I'm writing this book. I am writing it as it happened. From that moment on, I knew why I was back in the Castle. I somehow knew that it had its part to play as well. I couldn't help being excited about this offer, and also couldn't believe how it happened so quickly. About a week before I went to Enda the local paper did a lovely story on myself and on Tai-Chi and Qi-gong. Stella Carls of RTÉ picked up on this story. As she said to me later: 'Charles, everyone has a story, but yours is most interesting.' I still couldn't get my head around the idea that RTÉ was actually coming to my home in Kilraine. This programme was to change my life for ever.

I couldn't wait to go home to share the good news with my family. They were very pleased for me. My second-eldest boy, Peter, grabbed me and gave me a big hug, and said, 'It's about time.' It was as if he knew that this was going to happen. About a week before I appeared on national television, the local news paper did a story on me. That same paper told me a few years before that I was a man before my time. I was no stranger to the media, and not all that camera-shy. Perhaps to them, then, I was a man before my time. When RTÉ is in your living room, you somehow realise that your time has come.

All this hype didn't distract me from my real mission. I knew that this was just another phase in my journey that would pave the way for the future. It was time that I came out of the closet, and spoke openly about my work. The story on Nationwide went well, and even Grace got her say on national TV. When she was asked by the RTE interviewer what she thought at first about me doing the healing, she replied, 'I thought he was losing his marbles.' Her remark may have shocked my family, but it made me realise that she is my grounding energy, and that she, for one, wasn't going to put me on a pedestal. I am thankful to her for that, and appreciate that she always speaks her mind. I think her remark that day made the story more public-friendly, and kept the right perspective on things.

In the past I was very wary of the media but I somehow knew that this programme was not out to make me look like a fool. When I spoke to Stella on the phone I knew that she was genuine. Within a couple of weeks, RTÉ Nationwide was in my home. I was a little bit nervous meeting them at first, but after a few cups of tea everything settled down. Grace and I did very relaxed interviews that morning. Afterwards I did some Tai-Chi shots with some of my life-long students and friends over in the Castle, and in the Castle grounds. It was a really nice setting for the Tai-Chi display. Although my students got only a minute or so on TV, I wanted them to be with me and share this memory of my journey with me. I felt it was the very least I could do for them after all their support down through the years.

The programme went very well. Afterwards, when my father saw the video clip he said once again not to forget my granduncle, Dr Michael, who, he believed, was behind all this. I had a wonderful day with the RT É people, with Stella and her friend Michael, who was the cameraman. Michael spent the whole day filming around Kilraine. He took some lovely shots of the Castle, and of my home; even St Riadhain's well got a mention. Stella had promised me that she would do me justice, and I must say she did just that. I was quite surprised at the angle the programme took. Although all the subjects in which I was involved got a mention – writing, teaching and healing – it focused primarily on healing. Stella persuaded me to do a healing session on her, for the camera. When we were finished she was very relaxed and said to me, "whatever about Nationwide that was wonderful". I reassured her that you couldn't stage a healing, that it had to be genuine.

The most surprising thing was that after everything seemed to have settled down again, it was the teaching side of my work that really took off. That whole year was a remarkable year for me. I went out and taught Tai-Chi & Qi-Gong the length and breadth of the county, and outside the county as well. It all seemed to happen from the day of Edna's healing. Directly after the television programme, I had about fifty phone calls. The very next day I did a wonderful interview with Shaun Doherty, on Highland Radio.

It was my second interview with Shaun on Highland Radio, but this time it was a double-sided interview; I was interviewed with John Wilkey, a karate expert from the Letterkenny Karate Club. When I first saw John sitting there in his traditional karate suit, or gi, I thought the whole thing was going to go pear-shaped. How wrong I was! John was a very spiritual man, and a master of his art. He had nothing but praise and admiration for my teaching and myself. He said to Shaun, 'There is a great energy with this man, a great sense of calmness, I got it when he entered the room.' Sure enough, I remembered what Edna had said: 'Be yourself'. Although John and I were coming from totally different angles, Shaun managed to bounce us off one another. The interview went very well, as we seemed to complement each other at every turn. Looking back, I know that my guldes had their hand in this too; not alone in the interview, but in everything that happened that year, 2002.

14

Born Lucky

I had a week or so of media fame – I was in the papers, radio, and television, all in the one week. However, I managed to stay grounded and get on with the job in hand. Everything then settled down once more, and the phone got a little quieter. But, as a result of the media exposure, I was offered teaching courses all over Donegal, and outside the county too. I couldn't believe it. Before this, I would have to put posters up all over the place, and organize the whole event, but now, after a few minutes of fame, I didn't even have to advertise my classes any more. As luck would have it, I was asked to do a workshop outside the county, which took place on the 7th of April, just two months after Nationwide. I am a firm believer, and have been all my life, that nothing happens by chance, and that people only cross your path for a reason.

About a month after being on television, I got a phone call from a lady called Joyce, who was involved in Tai-Chi herself. She happened to see the programme on RTÉ. She wanted to know if she could meet up with me, and perhaps do some Tai-Chi with me. She was very impressed by the programme. I immediately agreed, and the following week she came to visit us at our family home in Kilraine.

My family home.

We had a wonderful weekend with Joyce, chatting about this and that, and doing loads of Tai-Chi and Qi-Gong. She had done the rounds with alternative therapy, and had a good background on the subject herself. She was really impressed with my style, I think, and really caught on to it. So on her departure, she invited me to stay at her home in Cavan and to give a day's teaching to her club there. It wasn't just the workshop that changed things; it was whom I met there. I indeed must have been born lucky, just as my mother often said I was.

I have some lovely memories of that workshop, the lovely drive down to Cavan that morning with the sun giving off its warm energy, recharging my batteries, to help me to do the workshop. It was unusual in that, about half-way into it, a few women broke down emotionally, as my healing abilities got through to them, and helped them to let go of old wounds and so on. At that time I seemed to be having that effect on people. A lot of healing went on that day, healing for myself as well. At the workshop there was a lady, who reminded me of the fortune-teller I went to see in my early years of searching. She said that "I had wonderful energy and that thankfully I didn't yet know how wonderful, but very soon I would, as things were opening up. It was a while, before I really understood what she meant by those words.

The other surprising thing about this workshop was that unknown to me, there happened to be a publisher among the group. Because I had written three books, but had nothing published yet, I was of course always on the lookout for a publisher and had been writing to them for almost eight years. As I was leaving the workshop that evening and saying my goodbyes to everyone, this lady walked right up to me and handed me her card. I realised that this was a publisher's card, and not that alone, it was a publisher I had written to a few times. I wasn't that excited. I called the lady back, and said, 'I wrote to you before.' She replied that does not matter, and that it had made quite a difference to have seen me in person. I was amazed. What's the chance of meeting a publisher at one of my seminars? Pretty slim, I thought. But as they say, nothing happens overnight. Later on we crossed paths again, just as I knew we would when I read the letter she sent me. Even though the letter was disappointing at first, there was still a lot of hope in it. It was this letter, above anything else, that kept me going; as I know people only cross your path for a reason. Her letter concluded: 'I am returning all that you sent me. I am still not totally convinced I am making the right decision, but I will have to leave it in the hands of the higher power for now. In any case, I hope our paths will cross again. I wish you and your family, and your work, all the best for the future.'

15

It Could Be Anywhere

I was very busy now, with healing, writing, and travelling all over the county teaching Tai-Chi & Qi-Gong. I was using the Tai Chi system, teaching people to heal themselves and grounding the energy in the areas I went into. Speaking of travelling, the summer of that same year, 2002, I made the biggest trip of my life, to a place called Fatima. For those readers who are not that familiar with the story of Fatima, here is a little summary of what it is all about:

The Fatima Children
From L/R: Lucia, Francisco and Jacinta

It was hard to think of myself going to a religious place like this. I thought religion was all there was to it. Normally it's the last place I would think of going. However, there's a reason for everything, and this journey had a major impact on my life and on my work as a healer.

THE APPARITIONS

On 13 May 1917, three children were pasturing their little flock in the Cova da Iria, parish of Fatima, town of Vila Nova de Ourem, today the diocese of Leiria-Fatima. They were called: Lucia de Jesus, aged 10, and her cousins Francisco and Jacinta Marto, aged 9 and 7.

About midday, after praying the Rosary, as was their custom, they were amusing themselves building a little house of stones scattered around he place where the Basilica now stands. Suddenly they saw a brilliant light, and thinking it to be lightning, they decided to go home. But as they went down the slope another flash lit up the place, and they saw on the top of a holmoak (where the Chapel of Apparitions now stands), "a Lady more brilliant than the sun", from whose hands hung a white rosary.

The Lady told the three little shepherds that it was necessary to pray much, and she invited them to return to the Cova da Iria during five consecutive months, on the 13th day at that hour. The children did so and the 13th day of June, July, September and October, the Lady appeared to them again and spoke to them in the Cova da Iria. On the 19th of August, the apparition took place at Valinhos, about 500 metres from Aljustrel, because on the 13th the children had been carried off by the local Administrador to Vila Nova de Ourem.

At the last apparition, on October 13, with about 70,000 people present, the Lady said to them that she was the "Lady of the Rosary" and that a chapel was to be built there in her honour. After the apparition all present witnessed the miracle promised to the three children in July and September :the sun, resembling a silver disc, could be gazed at without difficulty and, whirling on itself like a wheel of fire, it seemed about to fall upon the earth.

My aunt Eileen, who is also my godmother, visited Fatima quite often. Occasionally, she took some of my family with her. In 2002 she was unable to go and asked me to take her place. My brother Peter, my sisters Eileen and Mary, and my Aunt Rose were also going.

At first I decided not to go. Then one evening, after I had done a whole day's healing, I was sitting in the centre just thinking, 'What the hell would take me to Fatima? I had no sooner said these words, than I noticed an unusually sweet smell. It seemed like flowers, or the aromatherapy oils that Grace used in the Castle. I was totally taken over by the sweet smells, and a wonderful sense of peace. It was something so strange, that

My aunt Eileen.

I couldn't get my head around it. When I asked my son Hugh to come down to the centre his reaction was the same: 'Where did mammy get the lovely flowers?' He didn't take time to look around and realise that there were no flowers, or anything like that, in the room. After this unusual incident I realised I must

From L/R: Peter Shovlin, Mary Shovlin McBride, Charles Shovlin, Sr Rose Aquinas Kennedy, Eileen Shovlin Carmody

go to Fatima. I felt that the scent of roses was a sign from my guides. When I told Grace about the incident she was surprised. But she was very pleased that I had made up my mind to take this trip to Portugal. The next day, after I had finished a healing session, she smelt these unusual sweet smells herself.

A week later we were on our way to this lovely country. I had not realised that Portugal was such a beautiful country. I didn't realise, until later on, that Fatima could be anywhere. I didn't tell any of my family about the experience with the smell of flowers, except, very briefly to mention it to my sister on the journey, as she wondered what had changed my mind about coming. One evening in Fatima my sister Mary and I were out shopping. She picked up a rosary beads which had the same sweet smell that I had got in the centre just a few evenings before, a smell I could never forget. I told her this and she was just as surprised as I had been. That's all that was said. There were so many other wonderful sights, and things to talk about and look at, and other wonderful experiences to go through. On our arrival in Fatima I even got to carry the flag.

I must say I felt very privileged. But there was more to come. A couple of days later, just a few days before we were to go home, my sister and I were in the square.

We happened to see a priest, and I knew at once that he was a healer with very special gifts. So I said to Mary that we should go and receive a healing from this man. I felt it would be good for her sore back, and that I would get strength to carry on my work. She agreed. Apart from his piercing blue eyes – he reminded me of Enda – there was something else about him that caught our attention, his silver rosary ring. When I received the healing, he reminded me of the way I conducted my own healing except that he was humming softly, and he laid his hands fairly firmly on me. I thought this was wonderful, and very personal. So, from that moment on, my guides, who were still active in my life, asked me to lay my hands on anyone who asked me for a healing. They told me to give a healing to the family members who were with me, before we went home. They also told me it was not necessary to do the healing in the bare feet. This was a matter of choice. It was a test of my commitment, but, for now, I like healing in the bare feet. It helps me to connect to the energies. All these messages were relayed to me in meditation. In fact, I was so long in meditation that my sister Mary eventually asked me if I knew how long I'd been standing there. She said "it had been at least a few hours, and that we'd better be getting back, because the rest of the gang would wonder, where we were".

On our arrival back to the hotel, another strange thing happened. Eileen, my eldest sister, who happened to have been out shopping, came rushing into the room and said, 'Look what I got for you. I know you don't carry rosary beads, so I got you...' My heart jumped and I took a look at Mary, whose face had gone white. Eileen had bought me a silver rosary ring; identical to the one we had seen the healer priest wearing that day. When we told Eileen the story, she passed it off as a coincidence. But you know by now, that I don't believe in coincidences. I knew that this ring would remind me, every time I looked at it, about the blessing, and the strange happenings I experienced in this sacred place. Sacred, Fatima may be; but, apart from the olive trees, it is no different from the woods back home in Kilraine. I realised then, for the very first time, Fatima could be anywhere, and you didn't have to come to Fatima to be in Fatima, Fatima is in the heart. To me, it is all a question of vibrations. We can raise our vibrations by the power of prayer, thought or energy. After all, what is prayer, but the intention of thought? and what is thought, but energy? It's really that simple. So, you didn't have to come to Fatima to be in Fatima, nor do you need the scent of roses. Fatima can be present in the mind.

16

A Strange Happening

It was time to leave this peaceful place, which had changed my whole attitude to these holy shrines. I counted myself very fortunate to have been able to come to Fatima, a place of magnificence and peace. On the journey home, I couldn't stop thinking about it. My heart was drawn back to Portugal itself; I couldn't get over the quality of the people who lived there. They were, as my mother would say, the salt of the earth. I remember saying to my brother Peter, that if I had gone there in my early teens, I would have been very tempted to stay. The country, and everything about it, appealed to me: the lovely warm weather, the beautiful sunshine – but especially the warmth of the people who lived there. I was sad to leave, but looking forward too to going home and seeing my family again. I couldn't wait to tell them all about this place.

After I arrived home in Kilraine, I continued healing and teaching a little. Most of my time was spent with my father. He had just gone ninety-two and was slipping into poor health. A lot of my energy was devoted to helping him. My healings were, for the moment, somewhat quieter than usual. But that was all to change. My healings changed in an unimaginable way. The experience my family, my clients, and I got from the healings was out of this world; that's the only way I could describe it.

One day I was painting our fence, trying to catch up with some of the work that I had put off for the trip. A lady arrived, out of the blue, without an appointment. I was at the other side of the drive. I didn't pay much attention when the car slowed up, as I was engrossed in my work. It was only when she spoke that she caught my attention. 'I'm looking for a Charles Shovlin,' she said. I put down the paint bucket, and tried to wipe my hands a little. I knew that she was in trouble, and had come looking for a healing session. As she opened the car door and got out to meet me, a lovely aroma hit me. It got stronger as we walked into the centre. The lady said nothing until the healing was over. I never commented on it either, but it was the same smell Hugh and I had got nine days earlier. I knew it was definitely not her perfume. I was very taken aback but said nothing. Just as we finished the healing, the aroma got very strong indeed. It spread out from the healing room, into my little waiting room.

The aroma filled the whole centre with this wonderful feeling of tranquillity. The smell of violets and roses added strength to the aroma. As the lady got up to leave, she said, 'I hope you don't mind me asking you, Charles, what kind of stuff are you using to give off such a beautiful smell? You have the loveliest smell of violets, or roses, or something here with you.' I said I had no aroma of any kind. I didn't use anything like that, but I was glad she liked the smell of roses, because I liked it too. She questioned me again. I assured her I didn't use anything. By this time she was going around looking for some proof, even going so far as to smell the curtains and the furniture. Eventually she got a little annoyed, because I wasn't able to give her any answers. Finally she thanked me for the healing, and left, repeatedly saying to herself, 'Amazing amazing'. When the lady had gone, I asked Grace and the family to come into the centre, to see what they would say. The minute Grace and Daniel walked in, they were astounded, and asked, 'Where's the lovely smell of flowers coming from?' Grace believed it was the presence of Fatima, and the odour of flowers was a little reminder to me not to forget about it – as if I would. I felt this was going to be the last of this strange phenomenon. However, it kept happening, nearly every time I did a healing, even though some of my clients did not comment much on it. If they did, I just passed it off. I knew that this strange phenomenon was a sign _ that I was truly blessed in making that trip to Portugal. The aroma was Fatima's way of making its presence felt. I couldn't understand it myself, and I asked Enda and Sr Monica for their opinions. They both said, 'Just look at it as being a good omen.' I couldn't explain it and didn't even try.

17

Moving On

Over the past nine years or so I have learned to accept all the strange happenings I experienced, "and take them as they come". It wasn't all roses, as life is not so. However, we seem to manage between the reels, the ups and the downs of life, getting on with it. At that time my father was in very poor health and near death. Although I was well prepared for his passing, as we had said our good byes a few weeks earlier, when it happened it was still a shock. Still, I found I had an amazing strength and calmness that I couldn't explain. Even my best friend noticed it. She wondered how I was so composed and relaxed. At that time I had just given back the key of the Castle, giving it up for ever, because the owners had taken it over again.

Even though I hadn't worked in the Castle since the spring of 2002, I went over there from time to time to keep an eye on the place. It was time now to hand back the key, and move on. So, when the owners came for the key on a lovely September morning, I was only too happy to let it go. I'll never forget the relief I felt. It was as if a burden was lifted from my shoulders, and a whole new world opened up for me. I visited Enda a few months later, after all that had happened; my fathers death, – giving back the key of the Castle. He remarked, it was time to move on. It was time to give up the ghost, i.e. the Castle. It was after that visit to Enda that I understood, for the very first time, my own power. How else could I have survived opening a healing centre on a fairy fort? , I thought.

So today the teaching, healings and writings are going well. My guides told me that I would write only three books. I am on the third, so I think there will be less writing from now on. I don't really know what's in store for me. We'll just have to wait and see. We will leave it in the hands of the higher power or higher self for now.

As I come to the end of this autobiography, I want to reassure the reader that there is a higher power. It is within us, and it's important that we believe in ourselves. It's all about the choices we make in our lives – the energy we give out, and attract. These things determine our destiny. I realise now that what all those gifted people could see in me back then was energy, and the way I chose to use it. They could see that this energy is with me in everything I do. They understood that they were there to help me, as, being human, we slip from time to time. However, they realised a higher part of me was very much in control. That was what the fortune-teller in Cavan meant, when she said, 'You have wonderful energy, and thankfully you don't know how wonderful yet.' That workshop in Cavan brought it all home to me. If I had had the inner knowledge back then in the earlier years, I wouldn't have bothered with any of this. I wouldn't have gone searching in the first place. I suppose none of this would have happened. Now, because of my connection to my own source of power – a power that everyone has, I am getting my message across through my healing, Tai-Chi classes, workshops, books, and Castle Production videos. In 2003 I decided to publish my first book, Tai-Chi for Everyone. It was launched on November the seventh 2003.

So, the name of the Castle stills lives on, and it is never far from my thoughts.

Often as I'm pottering around, or working outside in the garden, I'll take a quiet look over at the Castle. I'll go over in my thoughts, how it all started. I think about how things might have been? if I hadn't had the wisdom to act on my inner thoughts , in Maynooth that day, the thoughts that inspired me to open the Castle and do my healing work there.

'The Castle' healing centre is the name I still go under and 'Castle Productions' is the label under which I publish books and videos. Looking back now, I see that what I really opened up was the dormant family trait of healing others in need. This means that I now see hundreds of people on a regular basis through Tai-Chi classes, workshops and healing. Today, I am not really searching for any big events or journeys in my life. I am quite happy to sit back, and take it all in my stride. I consider myself very fortunate to have found my niche. I am extremely thankful also to all those seen, and unseen, forces that have crossed my path and guided me on this journey.

Today, every time I think of that house, or use the name 'The Castle', I experience unseen forces. They are still with me, guiding me and thanking me for sharing this journey with them. It is the journey of self-realisation, of my past, present, and ever-changing future, that I have tried to share with you in the pages of this book. May those of you who buy a copy, or read it, share in its emotions, energy, vibrations, and healing - so that you too will find your niche – your own 'journey home'.

THE END.

The Castle Kilraine
Co. Donegal Ireland

www.The-castle.8m.com
charlesjshovlin@hotmail.com
~~www.taichiworld.com~~
www.tai chiIreland .net
www.Holisto.com

Other works by Charles "A Castle production"
Book "Tai Chi For Everyone" ISBN, 0-9545-7800-7
9-780954-578008
video "Tai Chi For Everyone "
also video on balancing the Chakras "The Seven Set Practice"

The Castle Taiji & Qi-gong,

Healing Centre

Kilraine, Co, Donegal, Ireland.

Tel. 074 95 51596

www.the-castle.8m.com

www.taichiireland.net

www.trafford.com

www.treasurebin.com

www.taichiworld.com

www.holistic.com

charlesjshovlin@hotmail.com

ISBN 141206602-6